Vulnerability Intelligence (Vi)

SET BOUNDARIES, NOT WALLS, AROUND EMOTIONS

BIPIN GUPTA

ISBN
Paperback 979-8-89744-680-3
Hardcase 979-8-89777-677-1

Disclaimer

The perspectives, quotes, stories, movie scenes, and references in this book are intended solely for motivational and inspirational purposes.

They should not be interpreted as definitive truths or taken as literal advice.

The author has carefully curated a collection of thoughts, experiences, and insights from various sources to encourage reflection and positive thinking.

While every effort has been made to present thought-provoking content, the author does not claim to provide absolute conclusions or prescriptive guidance.

This book is not intended to defame any individual, organization, or entity.

Readers are encouraged to interpret and adapt the content in a way that aligns with their own experiences and perspectives. The author acknowledges that each reader's journey is unique, and the insights shared are meant to foster self-awareness and alternative viewpoints.

Additionally, the publisher does not provide professional advice on the subject matter discussed in this book. The readers are solely responsible for making their own choices and decisions based on their understanding and interpretation of the content.

Dedication

To my successes, for bestowing conviction;
To my failures for keeping me grounded;
And, to my perspectives, for giving me the courage to
accept vulnerable moments in life.

Contents

Part 1: EQ Creates Leaders. With Vi, Those Leaders Create a Legacy

Part 2: Why Vulnerability Can Be Your Superpower

Part 3: Building Vulnerability Intelligence

Self-Acceptance Gives Us Space to Breathe, Sleep and Rejuvenate

Love is Absence of Judgement

One Negative Emotion Can Ambush Many Positive Emotions

We Don't Heal Emotions; Emotions Heal Us

Part 4: Supporting Someone with Vulnerability

We Need to Help Someone the Way They Want to Be Helped and Not the Way We Want to Help Them

Acknowledgements

If someone were to ask me, "How has your life been?" my answer would vary depending on who asked.

I would say to my wife or daughter, even in DIFFICULT times "Life has been full of love and joy, made by your presence in my life. You mean the world to me "

To God, I might say, "Life has been full of ups, downs, challenges, joy, and even uncertainties, but I am grateful to you for holding my hand all along."

To someone who has achieved great milestones that I desperately tried to achieve and failed even though I had skills, I would say, "Life is unfair"

My answers may differ, but all would be authentic.

I acknowledge that vulnerability, more than anything else has helped me evolve and grow. I have attempted to speak candidly about my experiences and learnings.

I thank everyone who has walked with me, encouraged me, and allowed me to grow through my vulnerabilities.

About the Author

When Bipin decided to leave the corporate world to pursue his social goals, his life took an unexpected turn.

Every project he initiated seemed to fail, starkly contrasting his past success, achievements and expectations.

His mind was fogged with self-doubt, shame, fear, and every emotion that makes one feel vulnerable. But, instead of giving up he chose to embrace them.

In doing so, he discovered something surprising: 'accepting failures gave him the strength to face them.' It reinforced his belief in resilience—the trait that carried him through life's most challenging moments.

He wrote his first book, *Failing Forward and Unrelenting*, in which he talked about his vulnerabilities, lessons, and experiences.

Beyond his journey, Bipin is an ardent student of human emotions and behaviour. He has trained in professional coaching (ICF), Emotional Freedom Techniques (EFT), and Neuro-Linguistic Programming (NLP), deepening his understanding of human potential, self-awareness, and transformation.

Today, he is a prolific author, writing on leadership, coaching, emotions, and team building.

He finds cinema to be a powerful medium for storytelling and reflection. He has thoughtfully incorporated iconic movie scenes throughout this book, making the reading experience interesting, engaging, relatable, and thought-provoking.

What Do the Great Wall of China and the Taj Mahal Have in Common?

Both were born from vulnerable emotions, whether rooted in love, protection, grief, or duty.

They transformed raw emotions into a timeless symbol of creativity.

Imagine, what embracing your own vulnerability could create in your life.

Prelude

I spent many years in the corporate world, worked with NGOs, and travelled across cities to attend workshops about human behaviour and emotions. I have always been curious to read about people who achieved emotional mastery, though I am yet to meet one in person.

I have had the privilege of meeting thousands of people along the way. And if there is one thing I have learned, it is that emotions have a way of showing up, whether we are ready or not.

Let me share about my learnings from first such workshops.

As I walked into that class, I saw tissue boxes and a water bottle under every chair. It seemed odd at first.

Water was okay, but why those issue boxes?

But within hours, I understood why.

'For wiping tears'

It hit me when I saw participants crying, sharing their personal painful stories, not because they were weak, but because they were finally letting go of emotions they had been holding in for long time.

Almost everyone, including myself, had a story—a vulnerability never shared.

Let me add that the participants weren't just anyone. They were well-read, educated, accomplished individuals, both men and women. The kind of people you would never expect to share even their private emotions in a room of strangers.

People shared their internal storms they were carrying deep inside them, like domestic violence, infidelity leading to marital separations, being abused by someone they loved or a perceived incompetence.

After sharing the reflections and conversations I realised that strangely everyone, including me, felt lighter and more at peace.

I saw that healing can happen, even when we share emotions with strangers. It is just that we need to be authentic, trust the process, and have the courage to speak out without fearing what comes next.

That's how emotions work.

My takeaways evolved my perspective on vulnerability.

Acceptance has the power to heal, but staying in denial can subtly amplify our worries.

Vulnerability may not be just about emotional pains—it can also be in our everyday struggles, the silent battles we fight within ourselves.

It can show up in something as simple as the choices we make.

Imagine someone, let's call him Robin, who wants to lose weight. He promised himself, "I won't eat sugar. I won't touch fried foods. I will be strong…."

But eventually, he indulges in eating everything that he vowed not to, leaving him feeling vulnerable.

Why does this happen?

Likely because Robin built a wall around his cravings—a rigid wall that confines his emotions. The human brain resists walls. When emotions are placed in the "forbidden" category, they don't dissipate—they expand and overflow from an outlet.

For the same reason, dieting often ends up with binging.

Now, imagine Rita, who also wants to lose weight; instead of starting with "I will never eat sugar….," she sets a boundary: "I will enjoy dessert on weekends, but I will treat myself to nutritious meals during the week." She doesn't deny her craving; she gives it a space and a limit.

Boundaries allow all emotions to coexist and don't let them bully us.

I will talk about Vi (Vulnerability Intelligence) in details later in the book, which is about being conscious of our emotions, understanding them, and not suppressing them behind the walls.

It is not just about setting emotions free; it's about being judicious about how we engage with them. Taking risk and trust.

Boundaries create space which can help to muster the courage to address vulnerability. To put it simply -

Wall would say, 'I don't trust anyone; only emotions behind the wall are safe.' while

A boundary would say, 'I will trust you as long as you are authentic and respect my emotions.

Let me share an experience about Vi. (Vulnerability Intelligence)

I worked with a demanding yet authentic leader. He pushed us beyond our comfort zones with tight deadlines and high expectations.

One day, my colleague Danish, an exceptionally high performer on the brink of promotion, suddenly quit. When we asked him why, he said he had found a better opportunity elsewhere. He left on a positive note, but the grapevine had a different story—he had felt uncomfortable working with our leader.

Weeks later, after a team review, our leader shared. "We lost Danish to the competition," he said. "I take this as

my responsibility. I will speak with him and ensure to bring him back."

He didn't elaborate on his earlier equation with Danish, nor did he defend his leadership style. But in that moment, he shared something deeper—his awareness of how he was perceived and his courage to acknowledge it.

While an outsider might not have understood the context of vulnerability in his words, but we did.

And yes, he did bring Danish back.

There are many leaders who, with a little more emotional wisdom, could become truly great.

As you read ahead, I request that you lower the walls around your emotions and explore different perspectives on Vi.

What is Vulnerability Intelligence?

If we add the word "intelligence" to any of the emotions, it might sound weird, such as Fear Intelligence, Anger Intelligence, etc. They don't quite fit, right? We are more used to lingo like Fear or Anger management because the emotions feel singular, distinct, and manageable.

But vulnerability is different.

It may not be just one emotion—it could be a complicated mix of emotions like fear, guilt, anger, shame, deprivation, jealousy, insecurity, etc., which again are braided together in ways that are not easy to define.

It can make managing vulnerability difficult as it needs a deeper awareness of it.

This is where Vulnerability Intelligence (Vi) comes in

It is not just about controlling emotions; it is about interpreting them so that they can respond with clarity and intention. It about being authentic when exposing ourselves.

Let me share more with an anecdote.

During my final year of college, like most students, I was preparing to step into the professional world. Back then, we didn't have the internet or easy access to career guidance.

Our decisions were often influenced by what parents or teachers knew as the best options unless we had some clarity. I was good at shooting and was part of NCC, so joining the

Indian Armed Forces seemed to be a good option. Besides, the uniform, discipline and respect that came along looked magnetic to me.

I connected with a few teachers who I thought could help with it. They broke my heart when they said, 'Wearing spectacles could be a limiting factor, and you also need to be able to distinguish between colours.'

While I was highly myopic, that last part confused me. I had never struggled with colours—I could tell red, orange, and green apart even with closed eyes on a lighter note. Why would that matter?

But, I realised it was not so simple; it was about distinguishing between subtle shades.

Out of curiosity, I took a self-test with friends, and guess what? I struggled to tell between deep blue and black and also between many different shades of colour.

This, they call it being 'colour blind'.

But How Does This Relate to Vulnerability?

It does -

What if the same were true for emotions?

What if we couldn't understand or clearly understand the emotions that make us vulnerable? What if we could not tell between the emotions and misinterpreted or ignored them altogether?

But the good part is that, unlike colour blindness, vulnerability isn't permanent.

It can be understood and addressed with Vi, which I believe that it is the ability to see the emotional blind spots. It is also about developing self-awareness, emotional resilience, and the ability to handle it without getting consumed.

The same emotion could mean different things to each of us, making it imperative to discuss 'what is vulnerability' so that we are on the same page.

Broadly, at work, it could be like a fear of failing as a leader or the self-doubt that comes with moving into a new role.

In relationships, it might be the shame of letting someone down, the tormenting gloom of a breakup, or the guilt of infidelity. On a personal level, it could be the frustration of being confined after an injury or the loneliness of feeling abandoned.

At its core, vulnerability is not just the presence of emotions—it is about avoiding expressing them openly. This may also come from a deeply ingrained need for safety, a fear of judgment, or the possibility of rejection.

Vulnerability can also be deeply personal. It's not just about what's happening; it's about how we perceive it. And when our emotions don't align with reality, things can get tricky.

We might have heard people say, *"You are unnecessarily getting hyper,"* or *"Calm down, it's not a big deal"*?

The truth is that what feels like an internal emotional pain to one could be less relevant to another.

Unfortunately, when internal pain becomes an internal storm, it can even get labelled as a "bipolar mindset"— which is a heavy term. Still, it could mean that unchecked emotional swings can distort our sense of truth.

But How do theories define vulnerability?

They say that it is a pattern of beliefs in which a person depends on external sources for validation or self-worth. This can lead to negative feelings about themselves and the world, particularly in stressful situations. It is an inability to cope with stress constructively, making the person more fragile or sensitive to it.

There could be a need for constant approval from others, a striving for perfection, or negative self-beliefs. It can be about finding it difficult to deal with life's challenges.

We often believe that the visible constituents or elements of vulnerability are the dominant emotions, like fear, guilt, etc., mentioned above. But the truth is, vulnerability is felt due to an imbalance between these emotions and the ones needed to address them, such as courage, gratitude, hope, clarity, acceptance, and resilience.

It is this imbalance that leaves us feeling stuck and overwhelmed.

The Biased Balance of Emotions

Let me share an anecdote.

My cousin, a married man in his early 30s with one child, had lost his job after his company shut down operations. His savings were running out as it took time to find a new job.

As weeks turned into months, he was building a sense of fear about the future, shame for not being able to find a job, guilt for putting his family in financial uncertainty, and frustration because of rejections.

One day, he got a call from an employer offering a good package.

He could not see any red flags when the caller asked for an upfront payment before issuing the offer letter. He paid for it.

Days went by before he realised that he was scammed. Now, he was even more Vulnerable, with intense levels of Shame, Guilt, Anger, Self-doubt and Helplessness.

These emotions were expanding his vulnerability.

What could have helped?

I believe that acceptance, confronting the reality of being scammed, hope, trust that better opportunities will come with perseverance, resilience, and the ability to stand rejection.

But we all know the hard truth, that what we see or prescribe as a third person is not normally seen by the person facing it in the same way. So, it could be easier said than done.

Yet, many find their way out, and I will discuss it later in the book.

It's intriguing how some emotions pull us down while others help us recuperate. It is a thin line.

When the imbalance crosses that line, it makes us feel vulnerable, and we get stuck, overwhelmed, or even numb. But when we start leaning into emotions that foster resilience, the shift happens.

We begin to see solutions, find strength, and move forward.

That is the superpower that comes with emotional balance—not denying vulnerability but using it as a way forward instead of a roadblock.

Now, take a moment to reflect 'What keeps someone vulnerable and unable to find their way out?' Here's what I've seen time and again. Maybe you've seen it too.

The Stories We Tell Ourselves

Have you ever caught yourself being hostage to negative self-talk? It's easy to do, and the tricky part? Our subconscious is naïve to believe that talk, believing whatever we repeatedly tell ourselves. I've caught myself doing it, too—until I tell myself to pay attention to the story I am feeding my inner world.

Let me share a powerful scene from the movie Jab We Met.

At one point, the actress, once full of life and confidence, starts blaming herself for being naïve.

She feels stuck, convinced that she made all the wrong choices. In her mind, she has failed. The problem wasn't who she was—it was the story she was telling herself. A distorted narrative.

When We Amplify the mistakes

Then there's emotional amplification—when we take a feeling and, consciously or not, make it bigger. This is especially common for new leaders stepping into their roles.

Besides, it could be all around us. We might have heard wisdom like, *"Money attracts money"*? Sounds harmless, right? But if one is struggling financially, that phrase could sound a BIG limiting wisdom. The same thing happens with vulnerability. If we believe our struggles define us, they only grow louder and amplify.

How We See Ourselves Shapes Everything

Our self-perception? It's powerful. Imagine a young athlete injured during practice. The doctor tells him, *"Most people don't return after an injury like this."*

At that moment, his vulnerability isn't just about physical pain—for him, it is more than that. Yet, how he responds to emotions could define his future.

The truth is that we all have stories, some that serve us and some that don't.

But the good news? We can always rewrite them. Vulnerability is not an enemy. It's an opportunity to change our internal dialogue, challenge the stories that hold us back, and be the version of ourselves we always wanted.

So, if I could ask, is there a story you might have been telling yourself? And more importantly— is it serving you?

Showing up Vi

Vulnerability Intelligence (Vi) is not about expressing emotions, it is about having the courage to be authentic. It's about accepting the fears, insecurities, and discomfort—not just hearing them.

I have seen that People with high Vi
- Express their emotions with clarity and courage.
- Acknowledge their need for help without shame.
- Own their mistakes and failures without self-doubt.
- Share their struggles without fear of judgment.
- Stay authentic, even when they feel exposed.

I have also seen how people's inner dialogues reveal themselves subtly from the way they talk during conversations. Like
- *I know it's easier said than done, but I can handle this with honesty.*
- *Am I the only one feeling this way?*
- *What actually matters to me at this moment?*
- *When I look back, how will I see myself in handling this?*
- *If I share my truth, what's the worst that could happen?*
- *I will face the consequences and stay true to myself.*

Brené Brown and Daniel Kahneman have both incredibly researched vulnerability and shared their findings with us. I find them exceptional.

Then, we might think that *Emotional Intelligence (EQ) and Vi are the same.* It's close, but there's a fine line.

EQ is about managing emotions—reading the emotions in the room, handling conflicts, and understanding people. It helps build relationships, resolve tensions, and inspire trust.

Vi is about accepting our own vulnerability, facing our inner fears, and standing in our truth, even when it's uncomfortable.

In my view, when we put them together, we just don't grow—we rather *transform*.

A Story of EQ, Vi

Let's talk about Akshay.

Akshay was a celebrated CEO of a large FMCG company. People admired his business acumen, leadership, and ability to manage tough conversations easily.

His EQ was exceptional—he could read people, de-escalate conflicts, and bring teams together.

When he was promoted to Managing Director and brought onto the Board, everyone saw him as an inspiration for success. What they didn't see was his internal battle.

Akshay was gay—a truth he had carried alone for years.

Even though times had changed and his identity was legally accepted, he feared misrepresentation. Would it overshadow his work? Would people see him differently? The self-found guilt was draining him.

Then came a moment of awareness. He realised that the person questioning his integrity the most... was himself.

One day, he chose to confide in the Chairman, whom he had always respected.

"I admire your courage, Akshay. Maybe Your team could learn from you about integrity," the Chairman responded after a pause.

That moment changed everything for him.

Later, Akshay experienced a huge cultural shift in his organisation. His team trusted him even more. People who once hid their own fears started opening up. His authenticity created psychological safety, and that safety became the foundation for growth as a team.

EQ helps leaders build trust. Vi makes them truly human.

When leaders combine both, they inspire teams and build workplaces where people want to contribute.

So, the real question is—how much of ourselves are we willing to bring to the table? Because when we integrate EQ and Vi, we don't just grow.

We multiply.

PART 1

EQ Creates Leaders. With Vi, Those Leaders Create a Legacy

Yet, We See People Hiding Their Vulnerability

Hiding or exposing could be contextual, based on gender, trust, social norms, relationships, and the intensity of a situation. Let's talk about them.

1. Gender and Relationships: Who We Share with Matters

I remember coming home from school one afternoon to find my mother unusually quiet. She gave me lunch like any other day, but something was different. She finally shared that my father's warehouse had been flooded due to heavy rains, making a large stock of no resale value.

After hearing this, I walked into the other room, where my father was watching TV. He asked about my day and talked as if nothing had happened.

Looking back, I now understand it better. My father spoke to my mother about his worries but chose not to share them with me, while my mother did. Men might see this expression as being weak, while Women may not. Beyond gender, this also highlights another reality—we choose who we share our vulnerabilities with based on the nature of the relationship.

2. The Fear of Judgment, Guilt, and Perceived Weakness

I had a close friend from my MBA days—strong, independent, someone I liked to be with. Years later, I found out through a common friend that she had been in an abusive marriage. I immediately called her, concerned and a little upset.

"You could have told me,"

She responded, "What was I supposed to say? Nothing matters now. Let's talk about something else."

Likely, it wasn't just about her hiding an abusive relationship—it was about the society that makes its own judgements. She didn't want to be seen as weak.

Think about scams—so many victims never report being scammed because they feel it may show them as naïve.

Vulnerability can carry a sense of shame, making people choose to suffer in silence.

3. Trust

People might choose to stay in difficult situations rather than open up. They believe that even if they do share, nothing will change—or worse, things might get more challenging.

4. The Safe space

People wait for finding one. They look a safe space to talk about it. In the #MeToo movement, for example, we saw how many people hid their harrowing experiences for years before discussing them.

It's heartbreaking to think of how much pain they carried in silence. The gruesome reality of hiding vulnerability could be a slow erosion of self-worth.

The longer we hide, the heavier it becomes, sometimes for a lifetime.

5. Acceptance

Some people don't hide their struggles because of shame or fear—they hide because they've convinced that nothing can change. Outwardly, this looks like resilience. Internally, it's surrender.

I've seen this in my friends who stay in unhappy marriages and colleagues who refuse to pursue their dreams. They build a protective shell, telling themselves,

"This is just how life is." But I've also seen others take the leap: a housewife who found purpose as a dietician, a woman who turned her pain into self-empowerment by working with an NGO.

Acceptance can offer temporary relief, but real healing begins when we face our pain.

Finding strength in vulnerability

Vulnerability is not new—it is as old as we humans. This emotion has been with us since we were born, but we have expressed it subtly in different words.

It has touched the lives of kings and queens with betrayals and revolts.

Hunters faced vulnerabilities against ferocious animals and calamities even in the Stone Age.

Failures, challenges, difficulties, and uncertainties have always been part of our lives; reflecting on these emotions is relevant to feeling happy, accomplished, and sorted.

Having said that vulnerability is often expressed in words like –

"I'm scared of what might happen next,",

"I'm not sure I'm ready to face it."

"What if I fail?"

"I can't do it; I am not enough."

"It is my mistake; I am responsible for what I have done."

These words reflect the turmoil of vulnerability—a state that, if ignored, mushrooms within, fogs our thinking and eats away at our peace. However, if we accept, retrospect and show courage, vulnerability can lead to finding strength.

I have shared workable ways to find strength in vulnerability later in the pages.

However, let me share real-life anecdotes that give me goosebumps on how people made this happen.

One of the most powerful stories of finding strength in vulnerability comes from the Battle of Saragarhi.

On September 12, 1897, 21 Sikh soldiers were defending a remote post against over 10,000 Afghan tribesmen. Outnumbered and without hope of support.

In that moment, which could bring down the courage of even the bravest of the brave, the Sikh soldiers chose to fight with courage and dare.

For about six hours, they fought bravely, prevented the enemies from moving forward, and killed hundreds of enemies before being martyred.

Today, they inspire countless others to find courage, even in vulnerable situations.

Vi is not about avoiding vulnerability—it's about leveraging it as a source of power. It's about understanding our emotions, disrupting limiting narratives, and showing our most authentic selves.

PART 2

Why Vulnerability Can Be Your Superpower

When Vulnerability Aligns with Compassion and Integrity, It Dissipates Uncertainty and Strengthens Our Purpose with Utmost Clarity

Vulnerability Intelligence (Vi) can help us find the core purpose of our lives.

Does that sound weird? If it does, let me take you through the following few pages and share more about it through my stories and insights, which might resonate with you.

When I talk about "the purpose of life," I'm not referring to financial or professional goals. While they are undoubtedly important, they may not be the core purpose of life.

I am talking about the deeper '*why*'—the reason we exist and about living meaningfully.

Without Vi, we often set goals based on what we think we know, but with VI, we begin to see beyond what we know, which can make our goals relevant.

It inspires us to thrive in the discomfort of the unknown, be authentic, and take a leap of faith.

Let me start with the great Indian epic, the *Bhagavad Gita*, which I believe most self-help books worldwide have roots in.

Mahabharat was one of the biggest wars in Indian mythology. It was a war between the Pandavas, who stood on the right path of Dharma, and the Kauravas, who were full of greed and deceit on the other side.

But shockingly, as the war began, on the battlefield, the mighty Arjun—known for being invincible and having incredible archery skills, put down his bow and refused to fight. He felt vulnerable.

What followed was a conversation that created history, changed Arjun's life, and inspired many to win their own internal battles.

Arjun and Lord Krishna (who was his charioteer in battle) exchange dialogues (the following conversation is not verbatim from the book and is adopted for the context)

Arjun: How can I fight against my family— elders, teachers, and loved ones? Even if they are wrong, how can this battle be right? My heart is full of sorrow and doubt.

Krishna: Arjun, your grief is caused by attachments. This battle is about Dharma, which is your duty.

Arjun: But harming them will leave me heavy with guilt. How can I justify this?

Krishna: You are not the doer; you are a part of a greater plan. Perform your duty selflessly without expecting the outcome. When your actions align with your purpose, the results will take care of themselves.

The outcome of this conversation was that Arjun was unstoppable as he fought the war only to win. All because his true purpose for Dharma was absolutely clear.

We can say that Vi gives us the courage to ask, "What am I missing?" or "What makes me do this?" and helps us move ahead and grow with integrity?

It opens doors to wisdom and clarity.

We have all experienced vulnerability at some point in our lives, and I am no different. Let me share my own experience.

When I was promoted to National Head in one of the organisations. I worked with the initial euphoria, which evaporated within six months. I realised that I was failing my team, struggling to meet expectations, and felt like I was becoming a non-contributing employee. With laurels, it was a feeling of being in hell; waking up in the morning felt like a loser, and dragging myself to the office drained me. I thought of resigning without any job in hand.

Finally, I gathered some courage to speak to my supervisor, someone I had known for nearly a decade from a previous job. He was a tough boss but fair and empathetic. Entering his office, I stood in front of him, holding a chair and said -

"I want to resign. I've failed to deliver or meet expectations." As I spoke, my eyes grew moist. Believe me, it was not easy.

He looked at me with no change in expression and said, "Okay, go ahead."

I was not expecting his reaction.

He spent the next five minutes discussing business status, not once doubting my capabilities. Finally, he ended the conversation by saying, "Now, please send me that report I asked for." He then put his head down on the laptop.

Walking out of his office, I felt a sense of relief. His subtle belief in my capabilities was evident. Later, he helped me tweak the business model, which was crucial and made a lot of difference in the outcomes.

I got back to work with more energy.

Today, if I look around, I can see how sharing my vulnerability helped me find ways that once looked like dead ends. I felt sorted.

I have shared about expressed vulnerability, but surprisingly, even when we perceive or observe someone with vulnerability, it can help us finding our purpose.

While we get clarity on life's purpose with Vi, collaboration with people when feeling vulnerable can also create miracles.

Vulnerability Intelligence (Vi) can manifest as **Visionary Collaboration**.

Even the world's finest leaders have demonstrated and set examples of collaboration to achieve unprecedented and create revolutions. The proof is all around us: collaboration in wars between the Army, Air Force, and Navy; the seamless teamwork of pit crews in Formula One, changing race tyres in few seconds; or the surgical precision in an operating room, where medics anticipate a surgeon's need for tools for a successful procedure.

Let me share another epic, Ramayan, an inspiring anecdote about the victory of good over evil. Let me share a less-discussed perspective.

Lord Ram was distressed and overwhelmed after the demon Ravan abducted Maa Sita.

We all would agree if I said he could have killed Ravan alone, but he deliberately chose to collaborate.

He built a diverse and extraordinary team united by a shared purpose. To name a few, in his team were Lord Hanuman, who could leap across the ocean and was invincible; Jatayu, a fearless, powerful giant bird; Warriors like Jamwant, a Bear known for wisdom; and Angad, known for strength and negotiation, Nal and Nil, who built Ram Sethu. All had unique skills. With him was also his brother, Lakshman, a great warrior, and even Ravan's brother, Vibhishan, who, despite being the enemy, was welcomed for his wisdom.

The outcome? Lord Ram's collaboration didn't just defeat Ravan—it also created heroes whose contributions we remember with reverence and awe.

Even our lives are a testament to the power of **Vi**. When one part of our body is injured, all other organs immediately collaborate to redistribute resources—blood, oxygen, and healing chemicals—to balance and heal.

While Vi can help us achieve our goals and collaborate, it can also help us win our internal battles, which may seem invincible.

Many years ago, my cousin Brinda, a brilliant and everyone's favourite family member, faced an internal struggle that is becoming slightly common among children and young adults today. She was obese, with a very high BMI, something that was visually evident. While being obese is not an issue, the struggle of being judged is.

Brinda was close to me and lived in Kolkata, yet she never confided in me about the emotional storm she was battling. Then, one day, I saw her in her new avatar. She had lost all her fat and was glowing like an angel. I was shocked, of course, in a positive sense.

I asked her, "You look lovely; how did you manage? Maybe it can help me too? She smiled and said, "bhaiya, I was just fed up with carrying the weight and facing the harrowing sight of people; I just threw my weight around on them until I felt revenged."

Of course, she was playful, using fun or, should I say, puns, and her expressions subtly recessed the ruthless emotions she faced earlier.

She told me that things changed at one point when she felt responsible for owning her life's decision to lose weight and took a leap of faith by starting one step at a time.

You might find it intriguing that today, she actually helps many to lose fat and gain health. She is a successful certified dietician and nutritionist, a great example of how people often find a purpose in life as they overcome their vulnerabilities.

At the cost of being repetitive, let me say that Vulnerability Intelligence (Vi) is transformative when handled with courage, trust, and integrity. But there's another magical dimension to Vi—' it is **Healing'**.

Accepting vulnerabilities empowers us to face illness with resilience rather than giving up with fear.

There is a connection between mind and body, often called psychoneuroimmunology. It is about how our emotional and psychological states impact the immune system. Hope, courage, and acceptance bolster immunity, while stress and fear pull it down.

Cancer is a life-threatening illness that can cause fear and make someone vulnerable.

It happens to many, even if doctors recommend a pathological test to rule out its existence.

Yet, there are many stories of people who've not only battled cancer but healed from it.

How did they do it?

Well, I attended a seminar on this, curated by a person who defeated the illness herself, defying death.

So here is the thing—She did take the medical treatment but changed her perspective about what was in control and what was not.

Her belief might seem unconventional and an imagination. So, she visualised in her subconscious that her damaged cells were being replaced by healthy ones and instilled a conviction in her healing power. She engaged with positive self-talk, embedding affirmations deep within her subconscious.

She accepted the illness but trusted the power to handle it.

But not every story ends this way—critical illnesses remain a big challenge—but even when the outcome is unknown, courage and trust can inspire the body in extraordinary ways when aligned with faith.

Healing also happens the moment we look our pain in the eye and say the magical words, *"It's enough."*

Let me share an anecdote. Decades ago, my cousin, a share sub-broker in Kanpur, suffered huge losses. For a sub-broker, one golden rule is avoiding personal trades and focusing on clients. But he probably got carried away. A poor personal trade led to mounting losses, and his attempt to recover through speculation added to the pain.

For months, he hid this from the family, keeping the self-instigated emotional storm to himself.

Before the pain and fear could become unbearable, he said those magical words, 'It's enough,' and mustered the courage to confront his fears and share the story with his father.

Things settled. His father was upset but could see that his son had learned his lessons the hard way. My cousin later got into the garments business and is doing well. He has healed from the traumatic pains of the past.

You know, people often say, *"Time is the best healer."*

But is it really?

The truth is, time does not heal—what we do with that time and how we deal with our emotions during that time make the difference.

That's where the Vulnerability Intelligence (Vi) comes in again.

It's about acceptance—being open about our pain rather than hiding it. When we acknowledge what hurts, we give those emotions the space they need to heal. It's not about agility but about letting them heal naturally, with patience.

And here's something I have experienced—it has this magical ability to help us see things differently. Sometimes, that shift in perspective we call a paradigm shift.

Let me share a powerful story from history—a story written on the walls of time. A king, the most powerful emperor in history from the 3rd century BCE, who expanded his kingdom, winning battles ruthlessly. Yet, he is remembered and respected for his transformation and wisdom.

We know him as Ashoka the Great.

After the Battle of Kalinga, King Ashoka looked at the battlefield. There were countless lives that had been lost, devastation led by his indulgence to win another battle. There were lifeless bodies of soldiers who had fought for him, dead bodies of the enemy, and even civilians. He was engulfed with guilt and sorrow, which he never experienced in life. He was mourning his victory.

His inner dialogues after Victory could be like -

"What have I done?" "I am responsible for it."

In one moment of facing vulnerability, he experienced a profound shift. He decided to own up to his act.

With Buddhism and a deep trust in his mentors, he transformed not only from a ruthless king to a Sage but also into an authentic being full of wisdom.

Why does Ashoka's story matter to us?

Because we all face our own battles—be it in relationships, professional careers, or personal struggles—we have learned muscle memory to hide our vulnerabilities.

But they are catalysts for the most profound transformations or a paradigm shift.

Let me give you another example. My friend's wife works at an old age home in Lucknow, and the stories she shares are heart-wrenching. Many of the residents have been abandoned—some because of financial struggles, others due to abused relationships or even bad intentions.

Unfortunately, their early days at the NGO could be filled with fear, guilt, anger, or confusion. They could be both physically weak and not able to understand why the very people they cared for have left them behind.

To many, accepting this new reality feels impossible.

But as days pass by, their perspective shifts. They let go of their anger and guilt and begin to find peace within themselves.

How does this happen? I asked her.

My friend's wife explained, "It starts with relationships they build with other residents, the staff, and even visitors. And in those connections, they find the courage to release their emotional pains and begin to heal. With new friends, they get the strength to face their fears, let go of guilt or shame, and move on to new phases in their lives. "

We have talked about healing and paradigm shifts. Let me share how Vi can be our strength to make a comeback.

Recalling an incident from school, we used to have debate competitions between the four houses. I was never chosen to represent my house; there were so many confident speakers, and I was a shy, reserved student. But every time I sat in the audience, I felt a sense of being left out.

One day, during a debate competition, the event teacher asked if anyone from the audience wanted to contribute to the discussion. Even after knowing that I could mess up as a speaker, I don't know what made me raise my hand. The teacher asked me to come up on the podium. As I walked toward the stage, my heart started beating fast; I wanted to undo it but couldn't.

I was kicking myself, screaming silently, 'What were you thinking, you idiot?'

When I climbed the stairs and stood at the podium, looking at the entire school, I went blank. The thoughts and viewpoints I had while listening to other speakers had left me alone, I guess. The crowd could have read from my face that I didn't have anything to contribute. I stood there, frozen, unable to say a word. After a few seconds, the silence broke into 'booing' by the students. Obviously, they were making fun of me. I blabbered something in response, feeling insulted.

One of the Speakers behind me—I remember his name—Ronojit tried to encourage me, but it was too late.

I had already convinced myself that I had made a fool of myself.

Luckily, my teacher asked me to return to my seat. I walked back without any eye contact.

Later that day, that teacher called me aside. She could sense the storm I was going through.

"You did something brave—many don't even dare to raise their hand."

I explained my reasons for volunteering and my struggle.

She smiled. "You know, Bipin, it's normal to freeze on stage. Many people feel the same way. One of the best things to do now is take a deep breath and confess that you are afraid to talk to so many people, say to the audience that you're nervous or not sure what to say. Honesty has a way of connecting with people. It just has to be real."

Her words stayed with me. She was talking about Vi, wasn't she? She said being honest with yourself in the moments that feel difficult can give you the courage you need. At least, that's how I see it.

Let me tell you something interesting, Vi can also help in **finding harmony.** Please allow me to elaborate.

If you have been to a wedding ceremony in north India, you have seen the live music bands that come with the bridegroom's family to the venue. These bands wear a rockstar-like uniform and add to the energy. Walking drummers, saxophonists, and other musicians create an environment to celebrate as family and friends dance their way through the streets.

They are often paid based on the number of musicians. But here's a little secret: during peak wedding seasons, when skilled musicians are in short supply, band owners might fill the gaps by dressing up random people who can't actually play instruments.

It sounds odd, but these "non-musicians" play a role even if they do not contribute to the music. They help create an experience. They sync their movements with the band, contributing to the overall vibe and energy.

Now, how does it relate to Vulnerability Intelligence (Vi)?

At times, we might feel like non—musicians struggling with a role we don't feel ready for or the expectations. Our instinct might be to hide from the centre stage for the fear of being "found out."

But what if, like those non-musicians, instead of focusing on what we don't have, we acknowledge the values we can bring with support?

Vi is about harmony and not about being perfect.

Building deep, meaningful connections—especially in intimate relationships—is considered a strength.

In my own life, while I have seen the incredible power of vulnerability in ways that continue to amaze me.

As shared earlier, men are often conditioned to hide their vulnerabilities, which may be due to cultural expectations. But, women seem to be more transparent about their emotions. They can subtly share their fears and anxieties and just presence by their presence, which could be through body language or expressions.

Let me share something personal. In 1997, I married a woman who found joy in life's simple pleasures and never asked for more than what I could provide. Even today, I tease her, saying, "I wish you become the same as in those first few years of our marriage." And with that loaded smile, she would say, "Well, you made me the way I am now."

And you know what? She's right. Back then, my life was more about work. Now, as I have enough resources, I try to make up for that with vacations or thoughtful gifts, but even those early years? They were magical with her. We didn't have much, but we had everything. A Rs100 meal at a local restaurant felt like a five-star buffet. Buying a tiny bell from a Christmas fair felt like treasure.

While she came from a family with multiple cars, a massive house, and a life of luxury. I had modest means—a two-wheeler and a rented apartment.

Yet, in her eyes, I was royalty.

But her vulnerability was evident in the way she trusted me, in the way she leaned in, even when there was ambiguity about things. Let me share more about it.

One evening, I came home exhausted and frustrated and said, "I don't like my job. I'm going to quit." With no job in hand and no savings—just raw emotions—she looked at me with eyes that reflected both fear and trust and said, "I don't have any problems, and I'm sure you won't let us have any either. I believe in you."

Her words exemplify exactly what I'm talking about, Vi—her trust, her hope, and yes, even her fear. Those moments can be life-changing for anyone.

While my wife and I are mere mortals, I believe emotions, no matter who they belong to, are immortal.

Again, while Vulnerability Intelligence (Vi) helps build deeper relationships, it also has the power to **transform fear into courage.**

Think about Adam, who genuinely loves Eve but is scared to share his feelings with her. He might regret the missed opportunity for the rest of his life. Maybe with a little courage, he could have lived happily with Eve.

With Vi, Adam could share his feelings and also be ready for Eve's response.

In our daily lives, most of us face small vulnerabilities—what I like to call micro-vulnerabilities—which only require micro-courage to accept.

For instance, I often see people not thank someone for small acts of kindness—like holding a door open or making space for someone in a crowded place. Similarly, leaders fail to express gratitude to their teams, especially when those teams are stepping out of their comfort zones to push for something greater.

Why does this happen? Maybe it's fear—the fear of looking weak.

I remember a therapist once told me, "The best way to get help is to simply say, 'I need your help.'" Yet, many people fear saying those words. The truth is, it only takes a micro-courage to ask for help.

While we have talked about how Vi can be our strength, let me share how it adds to the authenticity and trust anywhere.

I've had the privilege of working with leaders who express vulnerability in different ways like -

- *"I don't have all the answers, but we can figure this out together."*

- *"I take responsibility for where we fell short."*
- *"I'm on weak ground here, and the road ahead won't be easy."*

All expressions added to trust.

Let me share an anecdote from one of my previous jobs. In my team, I had a colleague in my team, managing a high-performing region, decided to resign. We had been colleagues for years, and I knew his decision wasn't about a better offer but about dissatisfaction with his annual appraisal rating. However, I believed the rating was fair and wanted to retain him.

On his last day, I called him into my cabin and said, after some general discussions, "Do you know that in your absence, I'll struggle to manage your team? Most are still new and learning, and I don't have the bandwidth. Would you consider staying a few more months to help me stabilise?"

To my surprise, he chose to stay. At that moment, I wasn't just his boss; I was human and trusted him enough to show my authentic vulnerability. And he reciprocated.

Let me now share about building Vi. I hope you find them resonating and interesting.

PART 3

Building Vulnerability Intelligence

Have you ever been stunned looking at someone with a well-defined, muscular body or shape and thought, *I wish I could look like that? Well, to confess, I have. Often. I did make an effort but ended up paying for a yearly* gym membership and going for just a few days. I was never able to sculpt the body I dreamt of. Why? Because I didn't put enough effort into it.

The same principle applies to building Vulnerability Intelligence (VI). Isn't it?

But here's the catch: while there is enough written and shared about how to train each muscle—be it exercises, diets, or coaches—vulnerability is a far less discussed "muscle" in our emotions inventory.

As you read the next part of the book, you might think, '*I already know this*. And that, my friend, is the point.

We often know the right thing to do, yet we get mixed up. Why? Emotions can be tricky, just like 'fear', which makes us feel safe and lets us to do what makes us feel safe.

Building VI is just like going to the gym: You push past the initial discomfort and, more importantly, you are regular.

Consider this: How do so many less affluent people beam more happiness than billionaires? Or how does an employee stagnated in the same role for years feel more sorted than a management graduate who climbs up the ladder quickly? The difference is what they choose to derive from the experiences that nurture their emotions.

As we talk about building Vulnerability Intelligence (VI), I have taken the liberty of sharing anecdotes and references to movie scenes from my perspective that deeply resonate with the context.

These stories and moments connect the dots between the context and emotions. I hope you find them relevant and maybe even inspire you.

Respect Vulnerability

I found a movie, 'Guru', incredibly inspiring.

A particular scene is very engaging. We can leave aside the exceptional dramatics and scripted parts. The lead actor, Guru, is put under scrutiny and questioned for his unconventional methods by a panel accusing him of violating laws. It could have been a vulnerable situation for anyone, but his response hits the bull's eye with rationale. He said in different words:

"I came to the city with no resources to do business. When I started, I learned the hard way and didn't know much about the law or policies. I did what I knew was right. I am a businessman; I see profits for my shareholders and myself. You can take everything from me, but not my conviction and skills."

He was damn honest and daring, admitting he wasn't perfect.

Most importantly, he was authentic and respectful to himself.

While this was on screen, we have a choice in real life, too — to respect our emotions and situations or let our struggles and challenges subtly dominate them.

Respecting vulnerability doesn't mean self-hypnosis to forget them. Rather, it's about facing them with courage and compassion.

I recall another scene, this time from the movie Trishul. In his journey from rags to riches, the actor plans to buy land from a rich businessman. He candidly says with pride,

"I want to buy your property and to be honest, I don't have a single rupee in my pocket."

That is cinema for us and perhaps a hyperbole on respecting one's vulnerability. But, a relatable example to showcase it with conviction. A person who has just lost a fortune in business can make a big difference in handling emotions when he says "I have lost everything but not my skills. I can rebuild business from scratch."

It might feel counterintuitive to ask why we need to respect vulnerability. Let me share more on this.

I once attended a workshop on healing pain conducted by an internationally renowned expert with a doctorate in emotional health.

We learned that many physical pains manifest from unresolved emotional issues that need healing.

In one exercise, we were asked to internalise and feel where the pain was felt in our bodies. But what surprised me was the next step—we were told to thank the pain and reflect on what positive purpose it might serve in our lives or what the intention of that pain might be.

Initially, this exercise felt bizarre. How could pain—something we hate and, at times, devastating—possibly add any value to us?

Well, the following were my takeaways after the exercise

- The pain slowed me down to let me rest in my busy life.
- It helped me receive attention and care from loved ones.
- It was a wake-up call for taking care of myself.

This taught me that even pain, which we dread, can have a purpose. Vulnerability is much the same. It deserves our respect because it offers transformative lessons.

Vulnerability makes us human, helping us connect deeply with our emotions and others. Just as respecting someone doesn't mean putting ourselves down, respecting vulnerability doesn't mean justifying weakness.

Showing respect could be as simple as just an honest acknowledgement. For a corporate leader, it might mean admitting to their team, "I don't have all the answers."

Relationships could be about sharing, "I am not perfect and have made choices that didn't work."

Respecting vulnerability could also mean owning it with courage and sharing it unapologetically with the world.

Respecting vulnerability begins with how we perceive it. Most of us grow up conditioned to hide our fears and insecurities, believing they make us "less competent than others."

To me, here's what respecting vulnerability could look like:

- Accepting that vulnerability is natural, and no one is immune from it.
- Being grounded enough to understand its messages about the limitations in situations.
- Creating space for it—just as humans coexist with millions of species, respecting vulnerability allows us to exist without judging ourselves.

Reflective Question:

Think of a moment when you felt vulnerable and questioned your abilities.

Please reflect:

- What were your takeaways from that moment?
- What could you have done differently?

Respect and Blame Are Inversely Proportional, when One Goes Up, the Other Go Down.

Self-Awareness and Self-Reflection

The storey line of my favourite movies (I would prefer not to share the name as it might take away the thunder) has a subtle stellar moment of self-awareness. The lead actor spends much of the time trying to communicate with his wife, who continuously ignores him.

His frustration builds until, in a moment of profound realisation, he sees the truth when he gets the self-awareness that he is already dead, having succumbed to an accident.

Moments of self-awareness in our lives could be eye-opening for many, as they show how we can sometimes remain blind to our own realities, influenced by external reactions.

That scene connects so deeply that self-awareness often comes in unexpected ways and can change the way we view life and ourselves.

It may need us to pause and look within, to question our assumptions about ourselves and the world around us.

We all would have been through emotional situations where we might have reacted differently from how people see us or place us as a person. At least, I have.

I have sometimes felt a tear or two rolling down my cheeks during intense scenes while watching a movie with my wife and daughters, who might not ever, seen me crying. I instinctively tried to hide those tears in the darkness of the movie hall.

But surprisingly, I felt more human and connected with myself as I accepted my emotions.

We may not have all the answers, but at that moment, we may feel self-aware enough.

Sometimes, understanding and accepting emotions may not need external validation; they can also bring a solid inner balance.

Let me share a moment that might sound hilarious from a ride on a crowded Mumbai local train.

Two men argued over a seat, which was normal in rush hours.

The first one snapped, "Who do you think you are—some kind of VIP?"

The second retorted, "Don't push; you don't know who I really am."

As the train moved, they disembarked at their stations like they never met.

But I found the comments of the second person with unintended depth.

How often do we, like him, assert that others don't know us—while, deep down, we may not fully know ourselves.

Every life experience brings emotions, and every thought shapes our perceptions. Over time, these emotions and perceptions influence how we see ourselves and the world. Left unnoticed, they can camouflage our real selves and our own emotions.

Even the most seasoned CEOs and accomplished leaders aren't immune to blind spots—hidden sides of their personalities. As a coach, I've seen how these blind spots can subtly influence decisions and complicate relationships.

Inculcating Self-awareness

Imagine a leader struggling with high employee attrition and feeling vulnerable in the situation. For self-awareness, he has to start with self-reflection from 30000 ft for a holistic self-assessment. He questions himself honestly.

- What could I have done differently to retain people?
- How do my people see me as a leader?
- Am I meeting the team's expectations as a leader?
- Do I need to get more skills?
- How can I build more connections with the team?

Each question peels back a layer of emotions, revealing the authentic self.

I saw an interview on TV where they had invited a sex worker to share her story. She was middle-aged and looked in her early 40s. I was amazed to see the peaceful expressions and calmness on her face.

She was very soft-spoken, elegantly dressed, and had a nice smile. She looked like a woman who could be a neighbour next door, someone we might know.

It seemed that, with profound self-awareness and self-acceptance as a human being, she had been able to overcome any vulnerabilities related to her profession. She even mentioned,' I don't have any problems if my daughter comes in the same profession.'

To share about getting better self-awareness and self-reflection

Let me share an anecdote.

Bhaskar had been married for just a few months, and his marriage was already in doldrums.

He found his wife to be unreasonably demanding and pugnacious to the extent she seemed mentally unwell to him.

One evening, after an argument over a minor issue, Bhaskar left home to take a walk in the open air and reflect on the situation. He realised it was high time he talked with

her cogently and straight and told her he could not handle her expectations and share his own limitations.

Returning home, he wrote down his thoughts, experiences, and how he saw her and her habits. Noting his thoughts was soothing for him, as he could reflect on them.

Thereon, while driving, daily, he used to observe his thoughts without judgement to realise that his own reactions during arguments were intense.

He decided to talk to his married friend, with whom he had always confided.

As his friend suggested, he tried putting himself in his wife's shoes the next day. He realised that 'He himself was too dominating during discussions, and she was just reciprocating.'

The anecdote may sound like it's leading nowhere. But like Bhaskar, we all need to put in efforts to uncover layers of emotions for better self-awareness, which could involve reflecting, journaling thoughts, speaking with someone, or being empathetic.

Self-awareness is largely a journey, not a destination. Each layer we uncover brings us closer to understanding who we are and how we can be a better version of ourselves.

Reflective Question:

Do you recall an instance when you realised something about yourself that you did not see earlier? What got this self-awareness?

Self-Acceptance

I find watching movies very unwinding. I see them as a reflection of society. Every time I watch the blockbuster movie Deewar, I find it inspiring. Leave aside the other stellar dialogues; one intriguing line resonates with me in the context as I see through my creative cinematic lens.

Please focus on the essence of this moment in the conversation, leaving behind the movie's plot.

In this scene, Vijay, who had become wealthy and successful, asks his younger brother Ravi.

"Aaj mere paas bangla hai, gaadi hai, bank balance hai, tumhare paas kya hai?" (Today, I have a bungalow, car, and bank balance. What do you have?)

Ravi responds in simple words, "Mere paas Maa hai." (I have mother with me.) Who had actually chosen to stay with him.

As I see it, Ravi did not brood or pay attention over what he didn't have.

He found happiness in what mattered most—his mother. Nothing else was important to him, and he took immense pride in that.

Actually, acceptance can be magical when done with astounding beliefs, particularly in testing times.

It is incredible that someone imprisoned for decades can return with a calm state of mind. We could not stay at our homes for a few months during COVID-19 because most of us saw it as uncertainty, anxiety, fear, and restraint.

We saw it as being contained, restricted or weak.

It is difficult to reconcile with the outcomes which don't go with our expectations.

Yet, during covid, people who accepted staying at home, stayed safe.

We need to find the balance with all parts of us that feel vulnerable. It could be an outcome of our destiny, wrong choices, mistakes, or even caused by others.

It also means accepting the imperfections without shame.'

This reminds me of the movie 'Todasa roomani ho jayen' in which The actress is always super critical about her looks and circumstrances. She meets a person who tells her to just say loudly, "Mai Sundar hoon" (I am beautiful). At first, she doesn't believe it—may be like a few of us? Somehow as she says it, resonating with the emotions, repeating it, experiences the magic.

It's not like her life suddenly changed or anything, but she learned to like herself just as she was. And that changed everything for her.

I could be repetitive, but we need to accept ourselves holistically, with all flaws, past experiences, current realities, and even distorted or messy emotions. Once we make peace with ourselves, we feel empowered.

People generally believe extroverts are the best speakers or leaders, but I once heard this amazing speaker who challenged this idea. She was talking about work-life balance, and during the Q&A, someone asked how she worked on her speaking skills.

She smiled and asked the audience, "What do you think—am I an introvert or an extrovert?" Almost everyone confidently guessed, "Extrovert."

She smiled and said, "Actually, I'm an introvert to the core. But it doesn't stop me from speaking up when I want to. Being an introvert doesn't mean I can't connect with people; it just means I have to do it in my own way.

If we look around, the most successful people are those who have accepted their weaknesses and focused on their strengths.

People who accept vulnerability are more empathetic and open to feedback, which makes them more relatable.

Reflective Question:

At the end of this chapter, let me share something from Mythology.

The Pandavas lived in exile after losing everything in gambling. Imagine their emotional storm, which could have included shame for losing their kingdom, tormenting guilt for putting Draupadi's dignity at stake, and frustration at not being able to show their strength as warriors.

What could have helped them to stay focussed in those tough times?

I leave this question for you to reflect.

Self-Acceptance Gives Us Space to Breathe, Sleep and Rejuvenate

Being Nonjudgmental

Often, vulnerability can be rooted in being judgmental toward ourselves or others. This can narrow the perspectives, creating blind spots and roadblocks to read emotions correctly.

Let me share how being judgmental can be detrimental.

In the corporate world, performance appraisals done every year to share a report card to all employees. They are often rated in categories like A+, A, B, or C, where A+ is for the top performers and C indicates below-par performance. Supervisors have to follow quotas (bell curve), meaning only a limited employees can be placed in different categories. Also ensuring that all are given a rating.

This often leads to situations where employees who believe they've performed exceptionally well might have to go with a lower rating. To a few employees, this looks unfair, and they fear being judged as incompetent.

Andrew, a hardworking and sincere employee, was rated B while he believed that he had exceeded expectations. Initially, he felt vulnerable and convinced that his supervisors were biased. Frustrated, he took a sick day to process his emotions and even considered looking for another job. But during informal discussions with colleagues, he realized that he wasn't alone—many high-performing colleagues had received similar ratings.

Instead of judging himself or his supervisor, Andrew decided to seek clarity. He scheduled a meeting, saying, "I worked hard and delivered on expectations, but I'm struggling to understand this rating. Could you help me with the areas for improvement?"

His supervisor shared how the category quota made him give that rating, yet he acknowledged Andrew's contributions and shared how he valued them.

Andrew, felt better even though not completely convinced. Yet, he felt sorted as he had made a discussion.

The Power of Letting Go of Judgment

Being nonjudgmental is about not making assumptions and optics. It is about listening, understanding, and making clarifications. This helps to see situations more clearly in moments of vulnerability.

On the same lines, there is something resonating about the movie English Vinglish. Shashi, a housewife underestimated by her family, finds her hidden strength once she lets go of the limitations created by others' judgments. She stops doubting herself and grows beyond her vulnerabilities with quiet grace. Her journey is an intestesting and engrossing story sharing that we don't need perfection in life, it is just about our readiness to work on our strengths without judging ourselves or others.

Judgment often arises when we make conclusions based on assumptions, biases, or incomplete evidence. Let me share a story which we might have read in school. A father, when returned home after work, out of anger killed his pet mongoose which had blood reeking from the mouth. He assumed that it had harmed his toddler in his absence. But when he found a dead snake in the room, he realized that the mongoose had actually protected the child from the snake.

His impulsive judgment came at an irreversible emotional cost.

We often judge people and situations based on surface level optics—appearance, speech, or the first impression. Based on these fleeting moments, assuming someone's worth or abilities is easy. However, when judgments are based on skewed perceptions, they lead to skewed outcomes.

Breaking Free from Judgment

One powerful way to break free from judgment is through open conversations. A simple question or an honest discussion can shift perspectives right outcomes. It's also about integrity—toward others and ourselves. When we are true to ourselves, we're less likely to judge others wrongly.

This is often a challenge that the team faces when it comes to getting appreciated for their contributions.

To address this, Leaders could ask questions like, "What helped you do it?" or "Who do you want to share your success with?"

To substantiate, let me ask you -

In Ramayan, who saved Lakshman in the battle.

or

In Mahabharata, who protected Arjun.

Well, most of us might say Lord Hanuman and Lord Krishna, respectively, for the two questions and would be right.

But the fact is that there was also a Vaid (doctor) who diagnosed Lakshman and prescribed Sanjeevni booti as medicine, which helped.

Again, it is said that, in the Mahabharata, Arjun's Chariot was protected by Lord Hanuman, who was sitting on the flag of his Chariot. As he moved from there, the Chariot shattered into pieces.

The point is that good leaders can be great when they go beyond the Optics and judgements. Behind Sales achievements, there could be operations, risk, HR, admin, or any team working in the background that added value to the accomplishments.

Reflective Question:

If someone you care about is being judgmental in a relationship and upset with themselves, how would you help them in the situation showing empathy and curiosity?

Love is Absence of Judgement

– Dalai Lama

Being Authentic

Let's talk about authenticity through a cinematic lens. Remember one of the most viewed Netflix series, Breaking Bad? There is a scene where Walter White, who was earlier a chemistry teacher, gets into the wrong company and a forbidden business. His wife is feeling vulnerable. But he looks at her and says, "I am not in danger, Skyler. I am the danger."

Chilling, right? But the reality was that Walter was not exaggerating or twisting the truth. He was brutally honest about who he had become. I'm not saying we should all go full Walter White. But there is something about that moment about being honest even when it is uncomfortable.

However, let me add that authenticity is certainly not about becoming an open book for the world in the efforts to be 'Real'. It is just about not hiding the truth when it is important. Imagine a leader going through a tough time at home and work. Does being authentic mean they have to share personal challenges at the workplace? Not at all. Authenticity is also about knowing what's relevant in the context.

It is about being transparent in a way that builds trust without intruding or oversharing.

It is certainly not about meeting everyone else's expectations about authenticity.

Here's another way to think about it—authenticity isn't just about the facts—

it's also about the emotions.

It's not just saying, "This is what happened"; it's about saying, "This is how I feel about what happened."

But again, it doesn't mean overexplaining, either.

Imagine visiting a doctor. You can share the symptoms you're aware of, but you might not be able to describe the ones you don't yet understand. That doesn't make you inauthentic—it just means you're sharing from your current awareness.

Similarly, authenticity is about expressing what's real to you at the moment, not about dissecting every layer of your feelings.

So, it also means sharing your truths even when it could mean a loss for you. Let me give you an example: investment opportunities. Statutory norms make disclosing the risks that come with investment mandatory, but that's transparency, not always authenticity. Authenticity could mean being upfront about what matters to the investor, even if it might make them think twice about investing. It could be about saying, "Here's the full picture, including the things many didn't like."

We all would have seen the advertisement of a product claiming 'no sugar added' or 'no trans-fat' in BOLDs. But they share in small fonts about what it actually contains.

At its core, authenticity is a balance between transparency and relevance, honesty and discretion, openness and self-respect. It's about showing up as your true self, not because you have to disclose everything but because what you do share is a meaningful reality.

Finally, let's bring this full circle with a classic Bollywood example from Sholay. Remember Thakur Baldev Singh, the former police officer? He had lost both hands to the villain, yet in a defining moment, he asked Jai and Veeru to help him seek justice. In the movie, he shares his vulnerability in a particular scene without manipulating the truth or hiding why he hired them. His courage and authenticity come through not just in his words but also in his emotions.

To conclude, being authentic could be scary to those who are yet to find that courage. However, it is okay to define boundaries when being authentic and real.

Reflective Question: Recall a moment when someone shared vulnerability that didn't feel authentic. What made it different?

Being Authentic is a Panacea for Healing Emotions Like Shame, Guilt, Fear, and Vulnerability.

Interdependence is Ok

When we think about interdependence as an option during moments of vulnerability, it may take some courage to share those emotions.

But, the truth is, sometimes, we don't even need to voice our dilemmas explicitly to feel supported.

Besides often just the presence of someone—or even something—in our support system can make all the difference.

This reminds me of two unforgettable, thought-provoking, and gripping movies that beautifully display the core of Interdependence: Life of Pi and Cast Away. In Life of Pi, the actor is stuck on a lifeboat in the vast Ocean with a hungry Bengal tiger named Richard Parker. The story subtly shares a powerful metaphor for interdependence. Pi and the tiger have an unspoken bond to face their vulnerabilities and depend on each other for survival and uncertainties.

Similarly, in Cast Away, the lead actor is stranded alone on a deserted island after a plane crash. With no humans around, he develops an emotional bond with a volleyball which he named Wilson and found it in the baggage.

These gripping narratives are a must-watch for those who want to see a side of emotional connections, how they work for us, and how they can add to our strength and resilience during the most testing times.

Both movies are exemplary examples of how our support system works.

These cinematic narratives are more than stories—they reflect the universal truth that we all need support systems in any way possible.

I have seen many youths not sharing their emotional traumas with parents, fearing being judged or even grounded without seeing their side of perspective.

It could be their learned habit and belief that depending on someone for emotional support is a weakness. The truth is that when this belief is broken, we feel liberated.

In the same context, I recall another award-winning movie, Good Will Hunting, which brilliantly discusses about it. In the film Will Hunting, a genius beyond the ordinary with a difficult emotional past, avoids opening up and taking help from others, fearing vulnerability. His life changes when he meets Sean Maguire, and believes him for making the big change in life.

This idea of interdependence goes beyond fictional narratives into our daily lives, where emotional challenges often mirror those faced by Pi or Will.

Many of us find ourselves trapped in a maze of emotional hardship, often getting into self-sabotage, feeling lost in a state of mind that might seem impossible to come out from. What makes this even more challenging is that there is no single solution for our pain—because we carry our unique story, a derivative of our personal experiences and perspectives.

There are some universal truths about emotions that we can all relate to. For example, fear and anger—can both empower or make us weak.

One thing I have experienced is how self-sabotage can show up in subtle ways: the thoughts we don't talk about, the assumptions we don't question, and the patterns we repeat without knowing about them. It comes from deep, unresolved inner conflicts and wrong beliefs.

Emotions will never leave us, no matter where we go and what we do. Imagine a girl named Annie who is left on the Earth as the last human being. How would she feel? Lonely, scared, and vulnerable. But we know Humans Make connections. So, she might create a bond with a dog or a bird. And guess what? That's not a sign of weakness or shame—it is about empowerment.

And that's the point, when we talk about interdependence.

Once, a father asked his son to take a bamboo ladder and climb to the second floor. The son returned, confused, and said, "There's no wall to lean the ladder against."

Factually, we can't do everything solo; even self-help has limits.

The ladder does not need to change at the heart of it, all we just need is to take a leap of faith, a little courage to lean it against the right support.

While we are humans; however, as per Indian mythology, even Almighty Gods show interdependence with respect.

Let me share the story of the demon Bhasmasura and Lord Shiva (we also know him for his might and simplicity). After granting Bhasmasura a boon that could destroy anyone he touched, Lord Shiva found himself in a dilemma when Bhasmasura wanted to touch him. The Gods do not take back boons once granted. So, he shared the complication with Lord Vishnu, who came forward for help. He cleverly tricks the demon Bhasmasura by disguising himself as a beautiful Woman and influencing the demon to touch himself on the head and face the consequences.

Let me sum up by saying that interdependence is a universal truth that exists in everything around us—cinematic stories, workplaces, personal relationships, and even mythology. It is not a weakness but a proof of our shared humanity.

We shouldn't stand there if we have a ladder but no wall in sight to lean on. Instead, we should look around and find a wall—a source of support to rise above challenges.

Reflective Question:

Can you recall a time when sharing or seeing vulnerability transformed a challenge into an opportunity? What role did interdependence play?

One Negative Emotion Can Ambush Many Positive Emotions

Stay Poised

What qualities come to mind when you describe someone as "poised"? Likely, you think of a person who is calm and composed in challenging situations, speaks only what's important, and shows resilience in adversities.

Yet, someone suggesting 'to stay poised' can feel completely opposite when overwhelmed or vulnerable. But, *it is important...* to express with authenticity and let the emotions do the talking. For example, if a sudden change in life has left us feeling anxious, it's okay to share that. If we are stuck in a situation, we can express that without tangling emotions.

In these moments, we also need to be mindful of what we share. Sometimes, even 'sharing less is more' because communicating our feelings effectively can be more consequential.

It reminds me of a touching emotional scene from the superhit movie Kabhi Khushi kabhi gam.

The scene is when Nandini shares her emotional turmoils in just a few words without saying one extra word. Even her husband is moved deeply to see her strength and vulnerability. We realise that Vi is not just about expression but about accepting pain and being heard.

When she says 'mera pati Parmeshwar nahi' hai and 'keh diya, bus keh diya' (my husband is not God, I said and its enough), she shows her vulnerability with strength keeping her poise.

Jokingly, my wife tells me the same thing in moments of disagreement.

I can't help but share another scene from the movie in which expressing vulnerability in three words made it gigantic.

Dilwale Dulhania Le Jayenge, the super hit movie, shared how beautifully staying poised can be so effective. In the film, Simran and Raj met on the Europe tour, where both enjoyed being together and got to know each other. Both developed subtle affections for each other; while Raj could feel it, Simran couldn't. When Simran handed her marriage invitation card after the tour, inviting him for her marriage, which was already fixed, Raj, at that moment, was not sure how to express his vulnerable emotions and how he felt for her. He simply said, "Main nahi aunga" (I will not come to your marriage). The answer was loaded with his vulnerable love for Simran and expressed in just few words.

This was precisely about how even sharing less could be more when feeling vulnerable.

We can choose to avoid oversharing as it may create unintended skewed comprehension.

We often weather an internal storm, confining it like water in the dam until one day, unfortunately, that water overflows in a storm, breaking all the barriers. And, when we finally share that internal storm with others, it may look like an exaggeration.

Why does this happen? Because we suppress emotions beyond limits.

During this internal storm, with self-awareness and acceptance, we can find a balance.

Looking from another perspective, emotions are infinitely expandable, and we cannot contain them until we inculcate another emotion.

So, if we feel vulnerable and fearful, we need courage, trust, acceptance, and support.

It's not just about vulnerability; it's about balancing the outcomes of emotions and the emotion itself.

Having said that, one of the most important things is to be resilient when showing it. It helps add authenticity and prevents you from getting overwhelmed.

And, how do you be resilient? In short, I would say by making conscious efforts like self-reflection, learning from failures, feedback, mindfulness, and gratitude.

Let me share a common example: The losing contestants might feel incredibly vulnerable after state elections in a country, as they had invested time, effort, and resources. Yet they say, "I humbly accept the outcome and respect the voters' decision. This outcome tells us we need to reflect and work harder."

If we remove any staged emotions, their statements reflect deep resilience.

They show acceptance, learning, and forward-looking emotions.

Let me add that when we are poised, we don't create threats to others and ourselves. We are actually building a safe space for expressing emotions and avoiding skewed expressions that could be misunderstood.

Reflective question—In the superhit movie Queen, Rani feels shattered when her fiancé leaves her just before their wedding. Yet, she surprises everyone by going on the honeymoon alone.

Besides staying poised, what inner strength do you think helped her handle her difficult situation?

Be Prepared for the Outcomes

Let me share an anecdote: Rajesh, in his mid-30s, lost his job six months ago. He believed he had been a victim of office politics.

He started his own food joint business with his savings; Rohini, a homemaker, trusted Rajesh's capabilities and contributed her gold jewellery to fund the initial capital.

His food joint business took off, and within a few months, he broke even. But before he could celebrate, something unexpected happened. Local authorities shut down his business because it was on unauthorised property—a fact Rajesh was not aware of while taking it on rent.

His shock and guilt were overwhelming. He couldn't tell Rohini about it. For weeks, he would just sit in the park as there was no shop, and he could not stay home. But Rohini sensed something was wrong; Rajesh seemed lost and quieter.

One evening, after days of sitting at the park, Rajesh gathered some courage to share the truth. He was not sure how she would react and also knew that she might not understand that it was not his mistake and feel upset about her jewellery, which was her only saving.

But he knew he had to share the truth, come what may.

He finally shared, "Rohini, I need to tell you something. The business is gone. I was spending time in the park of late, ...I have let you down."

Rohini sat in silence for a moment with a blank face. Rajesh was prepared for her reactions.

Regarding Rajesh's vulnerabilities, he did the right thing by showing courage and preparing himself for the outcomes. Fortunately, all went well, and his wife empathised with him.

The truth is that, healing can begin like a miracle when one carries vulnerabilities for a long time and musters the courage to share them with others.

Talking about courage to face the outcomes, let me share a scene where Jai in the epic movie Sholay when he was talking with his friend Veeru about catching Gabbar Singh, a feared dacoit.

Veeru says that he has already committed to taking up the dangerous task to Thakur Baldev Sing, to which Jai responds, even after knowing it could be a lethal decision, "Now that you've committed, we will see it through."

While we must be prepared for the outcomes once we have shown the courage and authenticity to share our vulnerabilities, it is ok to check if you have been understood well.

Imagine a Leader, Prashant, who has found a new opportunity in a different organisation and has to share it with his team, which is very connected to him. He is not sure if he has made the right decision, given that he has built a highly performing team that connects with him and trusts him completely.

He said, "I am not sure if I made the right decision, but believe me, I am sure you would do well even when I leave."

The team's reactions made him feel like an opportunist, and they did not show any positivity about his decision.

Now, Prashant can accept the reaction. But still can ask questions about what makes them feel that way and have a dialogue. If the team still feels that way, Prashant can choose to accept the decision and move on.

So, if the outcomes are unsupportive or misunderstood, it is ok to have a conversation.

To sum up, for being prepared and accepting outcomes we need empathy and respect for others' points of view and opinions.

Reflective question: How would you advise a friend who candidly proposed to his sweetheart, but it didn't go well? He now feels vulnerable, questioning himself, and struggling with the rejection. How would you advise him to process his vulnerability and move ahead?

We Don't Heal Emotions; Emotions Heal Us

Self-Healing

Imagine a person who, with great courage, trust, and support, leaves behind the vulnerabilities but doesn't heal the emotions that led to feeling that way.

Or think about what happens when a doctor treats only the symptoms of an illness without addressing the root cause.

In all likelihood the ailment will show up again.

On a very serious note, I feel this could be the most important part of Vulnerability Intelligence.

As mentioned, emotional pains can come back even more powerfully over time if left unaddressed.

Experts suggest that even most substance addictions start due to unaddressed emotions before they become pathological.

I can share my real-life example; I used to have alcohol for many years, and one day, I quit it not because I was an alcoholic but left it because I chose to. The researches show that pathological dependence on alcohol subsides after a few days of abstinence. Yet, I couldn't stay sober after six months of quitting it—not because of pathological cravings, but because my unhealed emotions that got me back into drinking.

But after self-reflection and a deeper awareness of my vulnerabilities that I managed to quit again. This time, I ensured of being more mindful of my emotions and how I interact with them.

I once read a powerful metaphor: A boat can sail across vast, endless oceans, making way in billions of gallons of

water. Yet, it can sink if even a few gallons get inside and have no way out.

Our emotions are no different. When we keep them bottled up, they bring us down. But when we heal them to flow with self-awareness and gratitude — we free ourselves to sail forward, lighter and stronger.

As share earlier, time doesn't heal; it provides space—what we do with that space is important.

Let me share my experience. A few locals misbehaved with us during a family vacation far from town. To keep my family safe, I chose not to engage and quietly backed away. We came back home safely without getting harmed.

For many years, I felt guilty for not taking action—maybe I could have at least gone to the police or sought help from others the next day. That guilt made me feel weak and less worthy at some level.

But now, I don't feel that way anymore.

Do you know why? Because I have forgiven myself. I realised they don't matter to me—my family does, and they were safe.

My takeaway? I had two. Firstly, I learned to forgive myself to heal. You free yourself when you let go of the guilt, regret, and blame.

Secondly, I learned to trust myself and others again, which helped me make the best of the times I spent with people I know and also the ones I don't.

Lack of trust might add to fear and self-doubts. And, to trust myself, I need to accept my imperfections and weaknesses.

I have experienced that to lose guilt, shame, or even jealousy, we need one simple yet very powerful state of mind: Gratitude.

Let me share my takeaway from Finding Nemo, a very engaging film that kept me on the edge of my seat. In the movie, the clownfish Marlin loses his wife and most of their eggs to a predator, leaving only one egg—Nemo. His love for his son Nemo becomes both his strength and his fear. But in their journey, something transformative happens. Instead of letting guilt and fear define him, he feels thankful for the son he still has. In that gratitude, he finds the strength and courage to let go.

While emotions like anger, fear, jealousy, lust, shame, and guilt often seen as negative, actually play a positive role in our lives. Each of these emotions has something to teach us, and if we can learn to have gratitude for all our emotions we Heal.

Having worked with NGOs, I found how magically helping someone with their pains can heal us. Working with a differently able individual or a child who lost parents with empathy can transform us into a better version of ourselves. It makes us resilient.

Just to add on a very positive note, any time I find myself perturbed emotionally, I tell myself, 'I am 55, and I know I have just a few more years to live if I go by life expectancy and am lucky to live that much. And the Life is too short than I might know.'

Somehow, I feel healed from any fear, anger, shame, or feeling overwhelmed in those moments.

Reflective Question:

Please recall a time when you had a misunderstanding with someone you really cared about. It left you feeling upset for many days. What helped you cope during that time? How did you finally find peace?

PART 4

Supporting Someone with Vulnerability

Do you recall any movie that became a cult classic years later but was not well understood when it was first released? I could be wrong but randomly, two films that come to mind for me are Lamhe and Mera Naam Joker. I still enjoy watching them today. The makers put their heart and soul into creating these authentic masterpieces. Yet, somehow, people failed to see that initially, not because of anything else but because the world wasn't ready to read them well.

Vulnerability is no different. No matter how real it is, it needs the right people to read it well, understand and support it.

Without that, it goes dismissed, ignored, or wasted.

At times, we even need to see them from different lenses.

Besides, when supporting someone, we need to remember that this isn't about fixing their emotions or proving that we have a better sense of what they need to heal.

The good part is that we may not necessarily have to be a psychologist or a master of emotions to understand their emotions. We just have to show up and be present in the moment.

Picture a mother with teary eyes. Who has recently lost her husband and is not able to recuperate from the tragic loss. Her 10-year-old son, who hardly understands what is happening, comes and says, 'Don't cry, mom. I am with you.' And wipes her tears.

What would that simple, authentic emotion make her feel? The world.

It just needs an authentic intention to be there for someone.

Whether we agree or not, the universal truth is that we all have been on both sides of the table and experienced how good or bad feeling vulnerable can be.

This gives us enough reasons to raise our awareness about what *they* need.

They need space to feel, process, and maybe figure things out for themselves.

They also need our trust to believe in them.

For example, imagine a leader feeling mixed up about a big decision they need to take. Instead of making brownie points with "Here's what people do in such a situation," we should try asking them, "What's on your mind?" or "How can I help?" or "I am with you." Sometimes, that much is enough to help them move ahead.

Or think about someone who's just been through a painful breakup in a relationship. Maybe they have locked themselves from the world due to guilt, sadness or whatever. You don't have to fix it. You don't have to cheer them up. A simple "I'm here for you" or "You can count on me" can make a world of difference.

This part of the book isn't about giving you a checklist for supporting someone. It is rather about brainstorming what it could mean to show up for someone when they're feeling vulnerable.

It is also about knowing that even if the situations are different, we can make a difference with empathy and resilience.

Look for Subtle Clues

Have you observed that when we ask someone, "How are you doing?" We get a similar response: "I'm doing great" or "All good".

I once tried an experiment. I asked ten people the same question, and they all had similar answers.

But here's the truth—sometimes, their response doesn't tell the real story. Behind a casual 'I'm fine' or 'All good,' someone might be wrestling with inner turmoil or personal demons. And yet, they still choose to say they're okay.

Why would they do that?

Maybe because that's how they want others to see them, or maybe they're hoping a well-wisher might look past their words, read between the lines, and see their challenges.

Or maybe they are not yet ready to show their vulnerability.

That's what makes looking for subtle clues imperative. Because –

Vulnerabilities Are Often camouflaged

Believe me, I've seen highly successful leaders feel vulnerable after questioning the status quo with their supervisors. They won't shout out about how they feel, saying, "I think I have made a blunder" or "How to work with a boss who can't tell the difference between right and wrong." Rather, they might try to prove that they are better leaders to their teams or unconsciously mirror the very behaviours of the supervisor they just questioned.

Research tells us that vulnerability can originate from 47 traits, such as remorse, procrastination, etc. This makes it imperative to understand the patterns—those subtle verbal, behavioural, or even digital cues that tell us someone might be facing their struggles.

Let's break it down.

Verbal Cues

People often show their vulnerabilities in the way they talk faking it.

Being Overly Appreciative

They might say something like, *"She's so beautiful, and her skin is like glass. I wish I were born like that."* Behind such statements there could be a story about their insecurity or low self-esteem.

Sharing Subtle Challenges

We might heard a distressed homemaker say things like, *"I can't do so many chores 24/7— and you are just enjoying life"?* It might seem rhetoric, but it could go far deeper when people take these words for granted.

A 'Please-All' Mindset

They might say, *"It's not that I can't say no to people; I just want to help them."* This sounds noble but can also indicate a struggle to set boundaries.

Behavioural Cues

When someone is hiding their vulnerabilities, their behaviour often gives it away in different ways -

Intense Emotions

They may overreact to small things, laugh too loudly at poor jokes, or need to hug people more often.

Avoiding people

I once noticed my cousin, who had faced financial losses, skipping family gatherings and avoiding people. It was his way of hiding his vulnerability.

Procrastination or Overworking

Some people lose focus, get stuck in their thoughts, or take forever to complete simple tasks. Even a few may get workaholic to distract themselves from what's bothering them.

A Changed Look

Sudden shifts in dressing style—like applying excessive makeup or dressing in a way that is not their usual style—can sometimes signal internal struggles.

Non-Verbal Cues

Then, there are the signs that don't require words or actions.

Physical Appearance

They might look exhausted, gain or lose weight quickly, or seem a little off.

Eye Contact

Avoiding eye contact—or making too much of it—can also be a sign of discomfort or vulnerability.

Digital Cues

Even in the digital world, human emotions can find a cover like -

Excess screen time

They might spend hours scrolling or posting, trying to hide their real emotions.

Emotional Posts

Frequent shares of overly emotional or overly optimistic content which could be a way of seeking validation.

Pseudo Happiness Online

You've probably seen those posts where someone looks *too* happy. Sometimes, it's real. Other times, it's an attempt to mask what's really going on. I am not sure if it does any good to the viewers.

A Story That Stands Out

This reminds me of the movie Taare Zameen Par (2007). In it, Ishaan, an 8-year-old boy, is misunderstood by his family and teachers. But his art teacher, Ram Shankar Nikumbh, sees the subtle clues.

He visits Ishaan's home, flips through his sketchbook, and looks at his vibrant paintings and creative imagination. In those colours and imaginations, he sees Ishaan's loneliness and emotions, which changes Ishaan's life forever.

When we pay attention, we can offer the support that really makes a difference in their world.

Why Should we really Care about the subtle cues?

Most importantly because it is about being Human and letting people know that they are not alone.

It doesn't just change one life—it changes families or teams.

Repercussions of ignoring these cues could be a wounded heart without hope, a family drifting apart, or a team feeling drained out in a toxic environment.

So, what can we do? Trust your intuition. Observe. Feel. Ask.

Reflective Question:

Have you ever found someone close to you feeling vulnerable? What subtle clues helped you read their state of mind?

Listening Without Judgment

The other night, I was watching a suspense movie with my wife and daughters.

In the film, an old lady was murdered in a suspicious situation when she was alone at home.

Her son unexpectedly came home from his hostel the day before, saying he needed money. During the investigation, it was found that he was an alcoholic and in debt to a local moneylender. Though he was crying uncontrollably, he became suspect number one.

Then there was the milk supplier—the one who first saw her body. He had a prior legal case for theft and looked petrified during questioning.

The housemaid? She'd left early the previous day and struggled to gather funds for her child's education.

And there was the tenant—a young woman who had conveniently left to visit her parents the day before the murder.

By this point, my family and I had engaged or put to work our inner detectives. We had each zeroed in on our prime suspect, complete with our own "reasonable" perceptions. But in the climax, when the actual killer was revealed—we realised it was the thief who broke in and killed the old lady as she tried to stop him—it left us connecting the dots.

Even in reality, we might also be quick to judge from the optics. Watching a movie is one thing, but this quick judgment happens in our everyday lives, too, doesn't it?

Someone doesn't respond to our text? They are ignoring us.

A colleague talks about their lavish vacation. Showoff.

And, interestingly —this judgment also extends to how we see ourselves. Believe me, we all do.

The Challenge of Non-Judgmental Listening

The universal truth is that the most challenging part of listening without judgment isn't just about others but ourselves.

If I struggle to learn something new, I might tell myself, 'I'm not smart enough'.

I might think I'm unlucky if I lose money in the stock market.

If I fail at work repeatedly, I may believe I am not capable enough.

Do these internal judgments impact our subconscious? There is no doubt about it, and they pile up, too. Before we know it, we've built a wall of self-doubt so high that it feels difficult to look at the other side.

What's subtle is that the same patterns of self-judgment rub into how we perceive others. It becomes like a muscle memory.

The Power of Story: A Lesson from Birbal

Growing up, I loved the stories of Birbal, a wise courtier from centuries ago. His cleverness and ability to solve dead-end cases are captivating. It's a brilliant read that I feel kids today might be missing.

One of my favourite stories is about a butcher and an oil seller who went to Birbal for justice, which goes like this —

The butcher, who visibly looked crooked said:

"I was at my shop when the oil seller came by. He was carrying a container of oil, and I was looking to buy some. I went inside to get my bag of coins to pay him, but as soon as he saw my money, he snatched the bag and tried to run away. I caught him and took it back. Now, he's claiming it's his money. Sir, it's all I have—my life savings!"

The oil seller, who looked poor and was equally agitated, said -

"Sir, I went to sell oil to him. He bought it from me and paid the amount. But when he saw my money bag, he got greedy and snatched it. I just want my money back, sir."

Now, at this point, most of us would've made up our minds about who was lying.

But Birbal? He just listened. No interruptions, no assumptions. He asked simple, open-ended questions like

"How do you usually sell your oil?"

"How do you keep so much money in the bag?"

"What did you need the oil for?"

Then, he came up with a solution that was straightforward and brilliant.

What Listening Without Judgment Really Means

Listening without judgment has two key parts:

Listening Actively

This is about going beyond words—paying attention to tone, body language, and even pauses. Sometimes, the real story is in what's left unsaid.

Holding No Judgment

This means holding back the horses before we jump to conclusions, asking open-ended questions and being curious, not fault-finding.

Here's a funny example of how being judgmental can backfire:

A friend of mine was getting ready for a party with his wife. She'd bought a new dress and asked, "How does this look on me?" Her eyes beamed with excitement.

Without thinking, he said, "You look slim."

Let me say he spent the rest of the evening without dinner. What he thought was a compliment ended up being judgment.

Back to Birbal's Story

Here's how Birbal solved the case: He asked the butcher to put the coins into a bucket of water. Moments later, oil rose to the surface. The coins, it turned out, belonged to the oil seller as they had traces of oil as he touched them.

No doubt the story ended with a brilliant note, but what stood out to me was not this. He could listen without judgment. He did not make assumptions which could fog his thoughts.

The Truth Rises to the Surface

Listening without judgment isn't about being perfect but being present.

You might read about the same context in different words as you turn the pages of the book because, it is the essence.

It is about creating a space where people feel cared for, heard, and valued.

When someone shares their struggles, consider holding the urge to solve, fix, or even label them.

Because when we let go of judgment, the truth rises to the surface, on its own, creating a safe space built on trust

Reflective Question:

What could change in your relationships with yourself and others if you listened without judgment?

Encourage Without Pushing

Let me start with a story.

Rahul, a Senior Manager at Raxe Bank, had been unusually quiet all day. Even after most employees had left for the day, he was still at his desk, leaning back in his chair and staring at the ceiling.

Tony, his colleague, saw him and stopped on his way out and said, "Man. Do you plan to stay late?"

Rahul turned his head, hearing the familiar voice, and responded with a pseudo smile: "I messed up again in today's presentation and faced the heat for it. It feels like my days here are numbered."

Tony pulled up a chair and sat down. "Tough day?"

Rahul looked at Tony as if he had found someone to share his pain. "I don't know if I'm just scared or if I'm really losing my conviction."

He shared more about his woes, keeping it short.

Tony said, "You know, my friend has these two cats. One's a bit of a bully—always stealing food from the other. The other one's quieter but agile, mostly trying to get along. They live in the same cat house."

Rahul could not make anything out of it and said, "Okay... and?"

"Well," Tony said, "I asked my friend, 'When they fight, which one wins?' You know what he told me?"

"What?" she sounded curious.

Tony smiled. "He said, 'The one I feed more wins.'"

Rahul leaned back again, trying to register what it meant.

Tony leaned forward and whispered. "Think about it— you've got two 'cats' in your head right now. One is fear, and the other is conviction. Which one are you feeding?"

Tony left with a pat on Rahul's shoulder, leaving him with a new perspective.

I shared this story because sometimes, to encourage someone, we might need to step back and simply hold Space for them. And it is not about a pep talk. It is about comprehending their emotions and letting them know they are not alone.

For example, saying, "It's okay not to feel okay," might seem a motivational talk to us, but to the person it might sound being judged.

Instead, they might want to hear something like, "I can see how you are feeling now after what all you have been through."

At times, they just need an acknowledgement.

Vulnerability needs Space

There is a difference when I look back at how my parents responded to emotions compared to how I interact with my daughters. While emotions don't change, culture does. Relations don't change but expectations, does.

For example, when I couldn't complete my Everest Base Camp trek—topmost on my bucket list—my father said, "What's so big about climbing a mountain?" Or when I was struggling after missing an opportunity, he'd say, "It happens. Get over it—you're strong."

But today, I can't have the same dialogues with my daughters; they might feel judged.

No pushing. No judgment. No Prescriptions.

We have to see people how they want to be seen

Here's something I've learned: Everyone's challenges and emotions are unique, and so are their needs.

I remember helping one friend through marital issues—it worked well, thankfully. But when I engaged with the same learnings with another friend, it didn't help at all. Why? Because I was assuming, not listening, not observing.

Sometimes, even asking, "What happened?" can feel intrusive. A better way to start might be, "Do you want to share something?" or "I'm here if you need me."

A Simple Trick for making them talk

My wife has a clever way of getting our daughters to open up. For example, when our older daughter started earning after completing her MBA, she often ordered expensive items online. If questioned directly, she'd get defensive.

So, my wife changed her questions. She'd casually say, *"Wow, this looks elegant—must have cost 5,000 rupees?"*

Validating that she made a good deal, proudly, my daughter would reply, *"No, it was only 1,500!"*—and just like that, we could know the real expenditure.

This same principle could be applied when supporting a vulnerable person. Instead of directly asking about their struggles, talk about something they feel validated or in control of.

Making Connection, Not Correction

Again, supporting someone isn't about imposing your perspective or rushing for solutions. It's about being present, being human and connecting.

Sometimes, just sitting beside them—without words, without judgment—is the most powerful thing one can do.

Reflective Question:

Which "cat" do you believe Rahul in the story above was feeding? What could he have done differently?

We Need to Help Someone the Way They Want to Be Helped and Not the Way We Want to Help Them

Showing Resilience

Let me start with a scene from Munna Bhai M.B.B.S., a movie beautifully showing how empathy can transform vulnerability.

The lead actor, Munna Bhai, whom I find a dude personally, and even had his poster in my hostel room during the college days, accidentally steps on a freshly cleaned floor being wiped by a janitor—an older man who likely feels ignored, invisible, and even lonely in the busy hospital. The janitor, irritated, bursts out with his bottled-up frustration.

A few might feel offended or insulted with the reaction for an inadvertent mistake or maybe even retaliate. But Munna does something incredible. He stops, apologizes, and hugs the janitor with Warmth and resilience—a gesture he named "Jadu ki Jhappi" (magical hug) in the movie. And, oh boy! This simple gesture transformed the janitor's emotions.

At times, when a hug may not be an option, a gentle touch, a word, or attentive ears can create the same magic.

Creating Space for Vulnerability

Let me share a story from Kanpur. A police investigation followed a theft in my brother's factory. They began questioning the security guard, a simple, hardworking man who was visibly nervous about the whole thing. The officer fired off questions, barely giving the guard time to respond before moving on to the next.

This could have been a normal process for the officer, but it left no space for the guard to explain himself—and, in turn, escalated his fear.

That moment made me reflect: How often do we unintentionally block others from expressing their emotions? Whether it's cutting someone off mid-sentence or responding with judgment—like "I told you so" or "You need to help yourself now"—such reactions actually block someone from processing their emotions.

When we show resilience by listening without any judgment and interruption, we encourage them to share more about themselve

Understanding Habitual Vulnerability

That said, vulnerability can sometimes become a habit.

I have an aunt who frequently cribs about her emotional struggles with anyone who gives her ears. People have even stopped paying attention.

I don't believe she might be staging a show, but she might need support in managing her emotions—perhaps through self-awareness or mindfulness. Even with her habitual vulnerability, she may still need help. It could be about a honest feedback.

Even in family WhatsApp groups, older parents or relatives often share the

typical 'forwarded' messages about feeling neglected, even when their children take good care of them. These messages sometimes seem vague, but they come from a place of vulnerability—a subtle way of saying, "Don't forget me. I'm still here."

What could be the best response? Showing Warmth and checking in more often, letting them feel loved and valued. Even when the solution is beyond us, simply holding hands is enough.

The Power of Patience

I once saw an emotionally touching scene in a retail store. A woman stood in a corner, hiding her tears. Her husband tried hard to figure out what happened, but she refused to open up, turning her head away whenever he tried to make eye contact.

Many feel that showing or expressing concern is part of supporting someone.

But then, he stopped pushing, stopped chasing her face, and waited patiently, giving her time and space. Eventually, she opened up. Although I couldn't hear her say anything, I could sense a 'shift'.

I have seen spouses lose patience in such situations, but to show resilience, we may have to wait while the person works through their feelings.

Yet at times they may still hold back from sharing details. This certainly needs patience and empathy.

My mother was born with that magical power of patience when we used to refuse to eat what was cooked.

What would she say?

In a simple tone without getting angry, 'OK, eat this when you feel hungry.' So, on a lighter note, now I was the decision maker, whether to eat or stay hungry.

Whether stepping forward for a "Jadu ki Jhappi," creating space for someone to speak, or simply waiting with patience, it is also all about what we don't do which is we don't judge, don't digress and don't rush. It is about being present and letting the other person find their own way to emotional sustenance.

Through resilience, we not only support others but also take care of our own emotions.

Reflective Question:

How would you suggest supporting a 10-year-old child who can't find his parents in the busy crowd and is continuously crying

Managing Your Own Emotions

We know how emotions can be contagious. When you're around someone who's happy or optimistic, it's almost like their energy rubs off on you. But then there's the other side as well. Spending time with someone who is fearful has self-doubt or is just overwhelmed can leave you with similar emotions.

While taking flight, we all would have heard this message: "In case of low oxygen levels, put on your oxygen mask before assisting others."

It is a simple but practically relevant advice for emotions as well.

Is the pressure okay?

On a lighter note, let me share an experience. After a tiring and consuming uphill trek that drained me, I decided to treat myself to a spa session. As the session started, the masseur kept asking, "Is the pressure okay?" Initially, I found it a little distracting, but then I realised how much it made sense for both of us.

This made me think about how often we check in with ourselves while supporting others. Sometimes, we need to stop and ask ourselves, "Is this taking a toll on me? Am I coming from empathy or sympathy? Do I need support as I support someone?"

It is okay to set boundaries, as it doesn't make us selfish; it makes us human.

The Shared Emotions

We all remember those early, harrowing days of COVID-19. It felt like the world was coming to an end. Locked inside, feeling vulnerable, we actually dealt with more than just the virus. The emotional toll of the pandemic was deep.

Taking care of ourselves was our first priority to ensure we were there for the families.

Moving ahead, If I had to talk about how I have experienced managing own emotions, three things would come to mind.

First, deep breathing. It is magical that something as basic as focusing on your breath can give you the oxygen you need to handle those heavy or negative emotions.

The second is mindfulness. This is about staying present and self-aware of your thoughts and emotions. It might need practice, but once we master it, it empowers us incredibly.

Finally, at times, imagining the situation from a third-person perspective can again help one become self-aware and gain a broader perspective on everything.

It is about respecting emotions, be they of someone you are supporting or your own.

Reflective Question:

What does taking care of your emotions mean to you?

Role of Emotions in Vi

What if everything you worked for was suddenly taken away?

I once read an interesting story.

A rich trader in a village had converted his huge life savings into gold and started feeling complacent, empty and without the joy he once had. He confided in a close friend and asked, "I don't know what has happened to me? Can you help me feel happy again in life without having me to go through the hardships of life again?"

His friend smiled and said, "Yes, I can. But first, show me the gold you worked for your whole life."

Trusting him, the businessman took his friend to his treasure. Without a word, the friend suddenly snatched a bag full of gold and ran away.

Shocked and enraged, the trader ran after him for hours—his heart was beating hard with fear, anger, and despair.

I am so stupid? He thought.

Finally, exhausted, humiliated, and ashamed of his act, he collapsed under a tree. He was filled with regret and helplessness.

But then, to his surprise, his friend reappeared, handed the gold back, and asked after a few moments.

"How do you feel now?"

Still recovering from shock, the businessman smiled and replied, "I feel so relieved. I feel happy, even."

Was the businessman vulnerable in this episode?

In the first view, he experienced deep fear, anger, and helplessness. But did he honestly face vulnerability?

Not really. Why?

Because he didn't have to deal with the real loss as his friend returned the gold before he had to face his vulnerable emotions.

He did not need to make difficult choices or show courage or other empowering emotions.

Vi is not just about feeling vulnerable—it's about facing it.

Had his friend never returned, the businessman would have faced actual vulnerability.

As discussed earlier, vulnerability is never one emotion—it's a complex mix of fear, shame, anger, self-doubt, guilt, despair, and other similar emotions.

And to move through vulnerability, we need emotions that empower us—courage, acceptance, gratitude, hope, and more.

I have discussed a few key emotions that shape Vi and how they can help us not just cope with vulnerability but also grow and learn from it.

Fear

John slammed his ice axe into the snow a few times before losing his grip on the left one. He felt relieved when he looked down. He had crossed the most difficult part, a vertical climb—an endless drop of ice and rock was all he could see below.

Then, he looked up. He said to himself, 'Camp 4 is close'. Taking a deep breath, he balanced himself placing both feet on a small, barely visible rock covered in snow and smiled before another rally of climb.

Most of us, hanging off a mountain like that, would be frozen in fear. But John wasn't.

Because fear is personal, it can be the outcome of what we've faced, what we've been told, and what we choose to learn or unlearn.

Think about it. As kids, we heard things like, "Don't talk to strangers," "Stay away from the edge," or "Failing is not acceptable, work hard!" But over time, these statements do more than just keep us safe—they build walls around our fears. And sometimes, those walls become so strong that we stop even thinking about what's on the other side.

We just keep fighting our fears.

But what if fear isn't something we need to fight? What if, instead of battling it, we just need to pull down that wall—maybe not all at once, but brick by brick.

Fear Has a Market

Fear, unlike many emotions, can be handled with courage. Few even make business out of it, too. Let's look around, public speaking classes exist because stage fear exists.

Many workshops, therapy sessions, and self-help courses exist for the same reason.

None of this is wrong. I have even attended many such workshops, too.

But it tells us that fear can have a price. People are willing to *buy* relief from their fears. And that relief comes at a cost.

But here's something to reflect on—what if fear wasn't something we had to buy our way out of?

Where Does Your Fear Come From?

Take a moment. Think about a fear that's stayed with you for years. Maybe it's speaking in public, taking a risk, or simply saying no to someone. But ask yourself—did this fear start with you, or was it passed on to you?

So, before we even think about fighting fear, maybe we should pause and ask ourselves -

"Is this fear mine or a learned behaviour?"

The Fear tense

Now, let's bring this closer to everyday life. Here are some thoughts we've all had, maybe silently.

What if I don't meet my office targets?

What if I can't express what I'm going through?

What if my wife doesn't understand my point of view?

What if I get stuck in a traffic jam and miss the flight or train?

What if she isn't happy with my decision?

And so on.

But did you see something common? Every one of these fears is about the future and what might happen.

The fear is mostly not about the past or present—it's about something that has not happened yet; it is in the Future tense.

Research tells us the most fears or apprehensions we have about things that don't happen at all.

So, next time fear finds its way, asking the following could help.

Is this happening right now, or am I just imagining?

What makes me so sure that my fear will come true?

What is the worst that can happen? What can I do to handle the situation?

Maybe fear does not want to harm us; it is just an alert or notification like we have on mobiles. It's a guide. It's the mind's way of saying, "Pay attention."

And, when we stop treating it as something to be fought with and start treating it as something to be understood, it loses its dominance.

Fear and Courage Can Coexist

The truth is that fear will always be with us in some way or another. Logic alone won't make it disappear.

Courage is not the absence of fear. Courage is having a fear, being candid about it, and doing what's important.

It is about not saying, "How do I get rid of this fear?"—but asking, "What's the smallest act of courage I can do right now?"

That's how you break the wall, brick by brick.

This chapter isn't about suggesting to "be fearless." That can be lethal and unrealistic.

Fear makes us human. Fear will always be there, just like courage will. The real question is: Which one will you listen to?

Sometimes, fear protects us, too—like during COVID-19, when the courage to live *with* fear kept us safe.

True strength is in living with both.

Guilt

Let's talk about guilt. Personally, I think it's an emotion that is often used in different contexts. When we hear a legal verdict about someone's guilt or innocence, it has a texture of crime. It may or may not have to do anything with the Emotions itself.

And when we mix guilt with vulnerability, it gets even trickier.

It could refer to something we regret—something we wish to undo.

But the truth is that guilt is about being in the past tense, unlike fear, which is in the future tense. Guilt keeps us stuck in what has already happened.

It can make people withdraw from the world or inside the shell. It is like an Implosion, which happens when a submarine goes too deep and external pressure is more than the submarine's ability to withstand it. The structure collapses inward due to the immense force.

With guilt the external pressure could be perceived as well.

Yet, on the other hand, when we deal with it on a positive note, it can also be instrumental in turning things around. It can even be a life changer.

And this is where great leaders stand apart when dealing with it. They don't say, "I feel guilty for failing my team."

Rather, they say, "I take responsibility." Or even, "I own this outcome."

See the difference? One keeps you stuck in the past. The other makes you forthcoming.

The best part? We get to define how we carry our emotions. We own them—not the other way around.

Guilt makes us human. A better human

The other day, I was watching a documentary about a serial killer who was finally caught and put up in court for taking many lives. What surprised me was that he felt no guilt during interrogation. That scene made me realize—guilt isn't just another emotion. It's what keeps us bound to our humanity. It can help us recuperate and heal, even when we can't undo the past.

But what if it is part of vulnerability? It may camouflage many emotions. One may start blaming themselves or others for everything.

Here, Vi comes into play, knowing that vulnerability isn't just about acknowledging guilt—it's about what we do with it.

It's about knowing when to forgive ourselves in whatever way feels right.

Maybe real courage isn't just facing guilt—it's sharing how we feel without expecting the outcome. Again, it is about being authentic.

A Thought on Healthy vs. Unhealthy Guilt

I had put on a few extra kilos and was talking to my dietitian. She told me to avoid unhealthy food—potato wafers, fast food—because add calories. She recommended healthy food like cottage cheese and egg whites.

This left me with a thought:

What if guilt, like food, could also be healthy or unhealthy.

Healthy guilt makes us to take responsibility and change for good. It can help us do better and be more mindful of our actions.

Unhealthy guilt can add that extra weight to our soul, just like unhealthy food.

Think of it this way: If guilt is like a meal, healthy guilt nourishes us, while unhealthy guilt is like junk food and leaves us feeling awful.

I thought about tracking how often I feel that guilt in a single day. So, I started journaling:

- Guilt for not going to the gym.
- Guilt for not doing enough for my parents.
- Guilt for not giving back a befitting reply when needed.
- Guilt for having that ice cream or sweet.
- Guilt for binge-watching a series.

And honestly? The list could be longer. But here's the thing— guilt doesn't make me a flawed human. If anything, it just makes me human.

So maybe the real question isn't about avoiding guilt altogether but how we see it. Do we end up hiding ourselves? or use them to trigger change?

The Spider-Man Lesson

Let me share a scene from the blockbuster movie Spider-Man. There's a moment early on when Peter Parker, who just became aware of his superpowers, watches a robbery being done. The thief is stealing from a man who had just cheated Peter moments before. Filled with resentment and vengeance, Peter chooses to look the other way.

But in a cruel twist of life, that same robber later kills his loving Uncle Ben.

The guilt makes Peter feel shattered —who wouldn't feel that way? But instead of letting it consume him, he channels it into something greater. He becomes 'The Spider-Man', dedicating his life to helping everyone against crimes.

The guilt may not have gone, but his actions give him a sense of purpose.

Guilt doesn't have to make us feel stuck. When used right, it makes that big and real change.

Closing Thought

Let me share something—I used to feel sad whenever I saw someone destitute on the streets, wondering what happiness could mean for them and why this difference between humans. I still feel the same way today, but over time, I've learned to channel those emotions into action in different ways.

And that's why I'm sharing this—maybe the answer isn't living with guilt but working on it while being real.

Let me leave you with a heavy question. A young, unmarried mother leaves her newborn child at the doorstep of an NGO. But she is filled with guilt and continues to feel vulnerable. How should she deal with it? Is her guilt making her a bad person, or could it push her toward something meaningful?

Self-Doubt

When we talk about self-doubt, the first movie scene that comes to mind is from the blockbuster Lagaan. It has a gripping story set in colonial India.

In the movie, actor Bhuvan, a villager, challenges the British to a cricket match, putting everything at stake on behalf of his village.

While setting up his team, he selects a player named Kachra, a man treated as being an untouchable. Kachra is visibly insecure and apologetic and doesn't believe he deserves to be on the team. But then, something happens. When he bowls with his crippled hand, his extraordinary ability to spin the ball stuns everyone.

He exceeds expectations in the match.

So, what made Kachra overcome his self-doubt? It wasn't just Bhuvan's belief in him—it was the leap of faith he took in himself. He performed beyond his potential when he committed to stepping beyond doubt.

Even at the workplace, when a leader says, "I am not sure how we will achieve this, but together we will find a way," he goes beyond self-doubt. He moves from self-doubt to trust and commitment.

At times, self-doubt, like fear, can also protect us. Neuroscientists link it to the prefrontal cortex, the part of the brain that helps in decision-making. It makes us to pause, assess, and make better choices.

However, when self-doubt gets amplified, people start blaming themselves for negative outcomes and attribute success to others.

How Self-Doubt Can Steal Opportunities

Sometimes, it can show in the simplest of habits—checking oneself in the mirror multiple times, seeking validation often or even how to deal with minor issues in life.

Over time, this habit can keep us from taking risks, and before we know it, we start blaming ourselves for not being 'good enough'.

I recall a Test match at Kanpur's Green Park Stadium. The final over, which India had to bowl, could have decided the outcome.

The Indian captain made a choice: he handed the ball to an off-spinner debuting in his first match. It was a golden opportunity. But what happened next stunned me.

The player shook his head—did not want to take the risk.

Eventually, he bowled. But I never saw him in an Indian jersey again.

Borrowing Conviction

I have seen one powerful strategy: borrowing conviction from other parts of life. Think about it—there are always areas where we feel in control, confident and sure. Maybe it's a skill we've mastered, something we don't doubt ourselves about. There could be self-doubts about talking on the stage or in a meeting, but we are super confident about writing emails or expressing our thoughts when writing them. When self-doubt creeps in about speaking, tapping into those confident moments of writing can remind us that how capable we are actually.

Athletes, leaders, and high performers all use this technique. They don't get overconfident in the moment—they draw strength from their previous successes. Just a moment of it enough.

And maybe that's the key. Self-doubt is not about ability but what we choose to believe at the moment.

Integrating Vi into Self-Doubt

Vi is not about living with self-doubt and feeling stuck in situations; it's about taking action.

It's about trusting that clarity will follow once we are committed.

It is about knowing that self-doubt does not help us with outcomes; instead, it requires courage, trust, and taking those first.

Vi is when 'Kachra' bowled even after his insecurities, the leader who did not give up in spite of uncertainty, and the missing link when debut cricket player who could have created history with it.

Shame

If someone asked me to share something I was ashamed of, it could be a difficult question to answer, but it would not take long. There is one moment from my early days in college.

I recall a girl on the passage leading to the exit—her head down, tears in her eyes—rushing toward the door. A few moments later, I saw a guy standing there; his expression made it clear that he had said or done something that had deeply hurt that girl.

Other students were eyeballing him.

I walked up to him with a concerned face and asked what had happened. He

smirked and didn't say anything. I stared at him, blabbering something.

And that's all I did.

I didn't push him. I didn't bash him up. I didn't make him pay for what he did.

Maybe I was afraid. Perhaps I thought I might get beaten up.

Or maybe I convinced myself it wasn't my fight.

But deep down, I knew I could have done more.

At that moment, I could not define my emotions. But I could not forget it over the years because what I felt was 'Shame'.

Whenever I watched movies where someone stood up for someone weak—where someone did what I didn't—I felt restless. My wife once saw my expression and thought that I was just flowing with emotions. But when I finally told her about that moment from college, she didn't react as I expected.

She didn't judge me.

She didn't tell me I should have done more.

She just cursed the guy.

And in that moment, I felt relieved.

And in that moment, I realised that sharing our shame is not about seeking forgiveness. It's about freeing ourselves from the noise that persists in silence.

That's exactly what Vi is about.

Today, I know that staying silent against a wrongdoing makes me complicit.

I know that acknowledging shame is the first step toward growth.

And I know that Vi is what leads past regrets into the courage to do better.

We often avoid calling a spade a spade—especially when naming our emotions. Shame is like that, similar to how my cousin called it.

I was talking to my cousin recently. She was working on a project with a group and had missed something during execution, something small but important, and was seeking advice. As we spoke, she kept repeating, "I just didn't see it. It was a mistake." I suggested a possible solution and added, "Maybe you feel ashamed for missing that detail?"

At first, she was defensive. But then, after a pause, she admitted, "Yes, I do feel ashamed for being naïve." And after that moment, she never brought it up again.

Shame often disguises itself as disappointment, frustration, or feeling left out.

But deep down, what we think is what matters.

I know this from my own experiences. I used to feel frustrated in school when I got bad grades—especially the year I had to repeat a year in the same class. I felt left out when I wasn't selected for a project and disappointed when I failed to complete an important task.

At that time, I defined my emotions as frustration, regret, or anger. But there was always a trace of shame, or maybe more of it beneath them all.

That's the thing—shame isn't always visible, but it is felt. It exists in life's small, everyday moments, shaping how we see ourselves.

And strangely, it loses its strength the moment we name it and accept it.

Shame can be revolutionary

As a child, I often heard my grandfather tell stories about his father—my great-grandfather—who had lived under colonial rule. He wasn't a freedom fighter, a politician, and was a simple person.

I saw a photo on the wall, a faded image of my great-grandfather. He wore a simple dhoti, white shirt, and topi, but his face looked expressionless.

"Do you know why he never smiled in pictures?" my grandfather asked.

"Why, Dadaji," I asked with curiosity.

"Because he never could, feeling oppressed, he had to do all kind of jobs before we got independence, to feed his family and keep them alive."

He continued, "You know generations before us were made to feel ashamed in their own country. But beyond a point, shame turns into something else. It can become anger. Anger can become courage. And one day, courage became freedom."

I looked at the photograph again.

I saw something beyond his expressionless face.

I saw resilience.

I saw the pain that was never expressed, the pride that was never claimed but passed on to generations.

I realised that vulnerability is not a weakness. It is about facing the truth, owning your story, and finding the strength to rise above it—and, in doing so, inspiring others.

When Shame is Left Unspoken

Allow me to share about the movie Deewaar, the blockbuster film starring my favourite star of the millennium.

In the story, goons tattooed Vijay's hand as a child: "Mera Baap Chor Hai" (My father is a thief).

Vijay grows up carrying anger and vengeance, knowing his father was a honest person. He gets into creating wealth by all means, be it right or wrong, making it a captivating rags-to-riches story for the audience.

Later, in a scene, his brother—an honest police officer, asks Vijay to confess his crimes and sign a document.

Vijay says with resentment:

"Pehle uss aadmi ke sign leke aao jisne yeh mere haath par likha tha."

(First, bring me the signature of the man who wrote this on my hand.) showing his tattoo.

Vijay's shame had now transitioned to an intention—an intention to never be seen as weak, an intention to gain wealth and to undo the shame.

His journey was compelling. His shame fuels his drive for success, but it also leads him to make choices that could define his outcomes.

While this is a cinema, in real life, when we let shame guide our choices, we risk becoming someone we never intended to be.

However, vulnerability intelligence is the way to deal with shame; it isn't about fighting or hiding it. It's about acknowledging, sharing, learning from, and, most importantly, refusing to let it write our future.

Courage

In one of the most loved movies, particularly by the youth, '3 Idiots', there is a scene where the actor, after completing his engineering degree, is sitting for a job interview in a wheelchair. One of the interviewers asks him how he ended up there. His answer shocked the panel—"I had jumped out of a window from the third floor"

That might sound like a sign of naive courage in a job interview. But wait, what came next was even more unexpected. When asked why he did it, he shared the truth that after getting drunk, he had urinated at the director's door and was about to be expelled.

Then, followed by an exemplary display of courage, the interviewers were stunned and uncomfortable with his frankness and straightforwardness. They said if he could change that, he might get hired.

But he said respectfully, "I have found my true self after breaking 17 bones"; I will keep my attitude. He was not afraid of the outcomes.

While, again, it is cinema, such courage is incredible.

Now, imagine a leader who just could not get survival funding after a presentation to the investors for his startup. How would his emotions talk if they could.

Anger – "Did they even listen? Or was their decision already made before I made the presentation? They are idiots!"

Guilt – "Did I miss something? Was there a better way to present this? My team trusted me with their future. Now, I am responsible for their future."

Fear – "How will I face the world now? Is this the end for my dreams?"

Self-Doubt – "Maybe they were right. Maybe I'm not a visionary leader after all. Should I have done things differently?"

Courage – "This hurts, but this is not the end. One rejection doesn't define me."

At this moment, courage is not the absence of fear or doubt—it is a call to move ahead even after knowing about the challenges.

Courage always has a precedent, just like the actor in 3 Idiots who once felt miserable or the leader who struggled to secure survival funding for the team.

Those moments of vulnerability can dissipate with courage.

However, jumping out of a plane for a skydive is not courage; it's fearlessness. Betting everything in a casino isn't courage; it's risk-taking.

True courage lies in acknowledging vulnerability and facing it.

How I see courage, metaphorically.

Imagine someone trapped in a car sinking into deep water. Panicked, his heart beating hard. Fear and helplessness are all in the air. The doors are stuck, the windows don't roll down, and anxiety fills the car before the water can creep in.

Then, in a moment of awareness and clarity, he remembers the hammer in the glove compartment. He grabs it, smashes the glass, and finds the way to the surface.

Courage is that hammer.

It doesn't remove fear, it doesn't make the water disappear—the car still sinks—but it gives him the strength to shatter what's holding him back and find a way forward.

Vi is the intelligence that helps us find and use that hammer in daily life.

Having said that, a spark of courage doesn't always lead to success, but it always leaves us with a lesson—like the time I stepped onto a debate stage in college yet couldn't find the courage to speak.

Courage is the first step to handling vulnerability. But courage alone isn't enough—just like breaking the car window was not enough to reach the surface. You still need the ability to swim to the surface. That's where Vi comes in.

Imagine a person who shows courage to share vulnerability often but doesn't learn to take the next steps to come out from it.

Imagine someone who often shows courage by sharing vulnerability but never works to go beyond it. Without next steps, courage can leave them feel weaker rather than empowered.

Courage in small, everyday moments makes a difference. The more we practice it, the more it becomes a natural part of who we are.

It could be saying 'No' when your plate is already full, staying firm when something doesn't align with your values, or even having the courage to admit a mistake.

Small acts of courage shape are enough to make our way.

Even a newly married bride moving into a new house with strangers might feel vulnerable. But when she takes that first small step—mingling, engaging, finding her place—she turns that unfamiliar house into her home.

Courage often comes with a bit of discomfort, and that's okay.

Let me share something from my school days— something I've never told anyone before. Honestly.

I liked a girl silently. One day, I finally gathered the courage to buy an Archies card, wrote my feelings inside, and personally gave it to her.

Later, she told me that the thing she liked most about me was the courage to hand it to her in person. That surprised me. She valued the courage more than the feelings.

Of course, we both got happily married to our respective spouses. It was just innocent childhood moments.

On a lighter note, I learnt from that experience that 'with courage, you can get what you want.'

The truth is that we don't have to sweat to build courage. We just need small, tiny acts—every single day.

Maybe it is a conversation you've been avoiding. Maybe it's a risk you need to take. Or maybe, just maybe, it's that one thing you know you should do—but fear is holding you back.

To sum up, courage is like that hammer in the glove compartment. It won't make fear disappear.

Courage will not stop the car from sinking, but it will give you a way out. The choice is yours—do you really want to break free?

Gratitude

Peter was anxiously waiting outside the operation theatre with his family while his pregnant wife was undergoing surgery for childbirth.

She had been in pain for days, and the family was deeply worried for her and the baby after the doctor mentioned some complications.

After hours of mental trauma, Peter and his family saw the doctor stepping out.

"Is all ok?" Peter asked with a concerned voice.

"Congratulations, both mother and baby are healthy," the doctor responded.

Instantly, the family expressed heartfelt gratitude to the doctor, nurses, and to the almighty God.

This sounds like a very common situation that we all might have experienced, but how does it relate to Vi and gratitude?

It does let me share.

We all show gratitude so many times in our lives, knowingly and unknowingly, but mostly when we go past our vulnerability. This is certainly important, but if we practice gratitude in everyday life or at least take moments to be thankful for few things during the day, every day, we will end up feeling less vulnerable even in the most difficult situations.

Gratitude acts as a silent antidote to emotional pain

We all have been vulnerable at some point. It makes us human, and we would agree it does not make us weak.

There are many people, things, situations, and surroundings we can be soulfully thankful for and show our gratitude to.

And we don't have to wait until we feel vulnerable to find reasons to be thankful or show our gratitude.

Gratitude is not a one-time thing; it's a way of being.

Many people make it a habit to find new reasons every day to be thankful—some even write them down consciously.

Just like we practice driving a car consciously on every move before becoming experts in it, we need to work on gratitude before becoming experts in it.

This actually is not an emotion but a habit or a part of our value system

Many studies and research confirm that people who show gratitude for what they have and are thankful for are more successful and happy.

Even in corporates, I have seen most successful leaders show gratitude for what they have achieved by acknowledging their luck to be in the right place for the right job at the right time.

In many homes across the world, families still sit together before dinner to thank God for their food. At times, I've wondered why everyone doesn't practice this habit of gratitude. I don't have the answer, but I do believe that a daily practice of gratitude can be a powerful tool for substantially reducing the feeling of vulnerability in different areas of life.

Having worked with various NGOs, I've met people who didn't choose their circumstances—some were abandoned by family, some were differently abled, and some never even knew their parents. Yet, facing their challenges, they show immense gratitude to those who visit and spend time with them.

This is Vulnerability Intelligence (Vi) in action.

They may still have some of their emotional wounds, but their gratitude helps them shift focus from what is not there to what is there.

I invite you to join me and take a moment to reflect even as you read this book. We both have endless reasons to be grateful—some we acknowledge and many more we've never even paid attention to.

Consciously redirecting our attention to what we can be grateful for can shift our emotional state. It doesn't have to be something extraordinary—it could be as simple as:

We are breathing; you are able to read this, and I am able to write.

We have a home to return to in the evening.

We have family and friends who support us.

Or that even the hope of a better tomorrow.

Even in moments of despair, we know a guiding force around us has been taking care of us.

And so much more.

For a moment, let me switch to my left brain— the logical, mathematical side of thinking

Imagine our consciousness and subconsciousness together add up to 1.

This makes our complete unit of awareness.

When we feel vulnerable, our fears, doubts, and emotions consume a portion, x, of our awareness.

This leaves (1-x) of our awareness available—still holding space for gratitude.

And that could be enough antidote to dilute the value of X.

To sum up, while we practice gratitude, it is good to be authentic about emotions. This means knowing that it is ok to feel vulnerable while showing gratitude.

Gratitude doesn't erase vulnerability, but it dilutes it.

So, where we choose to place our awareness is our choice.

Forgiveness

It's funny how we believe that we have moved on from resenting something, only to realise years later that we are still carrying it—like an old pain, anger, or hurt—just waiting for the right time to pull us down.

I have learned from people who have actually learned about human emotions that we often ignore how much of this baggage comes from childhood. We grow up and get busy with our lives, but those emotions? They stay with us, sometimes avoided and sometimes even fed to make it bigger.

While being part of one of the workshops on Emotional mastery, I worked with a lady who had subtle troubling memories from her childhood; she was angry at her parents because she felt they hadn't cared for her the way she expected and they could.

Here is something important about emotions: whether she was right or wrong in her judgment is never a point.

Her emotions felt real to her. That mattered. And she was not able to forgive her parents.

And then I learned something powerful.

She closed her eyes, took a deep breath, and imagined herself going back to her childhood in her current grown-up version to the time when she felt like ignored and hurt. She visualised meeting her younger self face-to-face. She lovingly sat with her, listened to her pain, and gently assured her that she was not alone, besides other things. And, made her see the larger picture.

After her visualisations, she felt healed and lighter when she opened her eyes. She had forgiven her parents for how she felt. She felt healed.

That's the thing about forgiveness.

It's not about ignoring pain. It's about grieving and understanding it and then releasing it when you are ready.

Forgiving someone just because we *should*, because it's the "right thing to do," doesn't set us free.

Vi isn't about camouflaging emotions. It's about being authentic with emotions, feeling them, and being kind to yourself.

So, How Do We Move Beyond the Pain?

I know—it may sound strange. How can you possibly be grateful when someone hurts you? But gratitude has its own way of shifting our focus—from what was taken from us to what we still have.

I once met an elderly man at an old age home. His family had abandoned him *when he fell ill, and for days, he carried deep resentment. And honestly, who would not stand with him, such a gentleman? Anyone who listened to his sad story could feel his emotions.*

But something changed after a few days.

Instead of talking about those who had left him, he slowly talked about what was going well in his life now. He was grateful for the kindness of the strangers who ran the home, for the meals, and for the simple warmth of others who stayed there. He was thanking God more than ever before. I don't know if he had forgiven his family, but they didn't matter to him now.

And that's about **forgiveness**—gratitude walks along with it.

We don't forgive because the other person deserves it. We forgive because **we deserve peace.**

When we forgive someone, we do it from a position of strength and clarity. This strength and clarity come with gratitude.

The Power of Letting It Go

Let me share another workshop exercise that really stayed with me. It was one of the most unexpectedly powerful methods of forgiveness I've ever experienced.

Participants were split into pairs and asked to share a personal story of anger that still held them back—something they couldn't shake off.

They were urged to say every damn thing they had bottled up. This could even spiced up with abuses if they needed to. But you know what? Even after all that, many still had some anger left.

The next step? Physical release.

They were given safe ways to externalise their emotions—hitting a chair, screaming into a pillow, tearing up paper. It sounds strange, maybe even a little silly. And then, something happened.

As people physically expressed their anger, their bottled-up emotions were gone, largely. It wasn't just about *forgiveness.* It was about *allowing the subconscious* to process the emotions it had been holding onto for so long.

This reminds me of that scene in my favourite, exceptional movie, Jab We Met. The actor blames the world, besides the girl whom he liked but had ditched him.

The actress asked him to burn this girl's photo, which he was still carrying in his wallet.

She then asks him to flush it in the toilet after burning it, believing that he is flushing her out of his life. The actor, who initially found this act absurd, found that it actually made him feel better.

The Most Important Part of Forgiveness

We talk about forgiving others.

But what about forgiving ourselves?

I have met people who punish themselves for past decisions and behaviours. Some stay with guilt and a few get into addictions.

We often forget that there is no one is without flaws and it is human to make mistakes. Authentic regret should lead to a better version of oneself, not vulnerability. But yes, as mentioned earlier grieving the mistake before forgiveness makes it authentic.

Forgiving yourself isn't about deleting the past.

It's about acknowledging, learning, and moving forward without self-sabotage.

Forgiveness is the Ultimate Act of Power

Not because it lets someone else off the hook.

But because it sets YOU free.

Hope

If hope is '1' at its peak, what would it be at its lowest possible value?

Many might instinctively say '0'—when all hope is lost.

But I respectfully disagree.

Hope never can be zero as long as we are alive. Well, that's my view and perspective.

It is about believing that something still matters, even when nothing makes sense.

And as long as something matters, hope will never be zero.

Even a terminally ill person, who may have no hope for survival, might still hope for their family's well-being, for a peaceful farewell, or for being remembered well or something else.

Hope has no true antonym

Not even vulnerability, which actually stands at the cusp of courage. When we are vulnerable, we need the courage to show ourselves authentically—to express how we feel.

And to find that courage, we need hope—hope that we will be accepted, or taking that the risk is worth it.

Few stories personify hope. In the gripping, must-watch movie The Shawshank Redemption, in which the actor is imprisoned for years but never gives up or allows despair make him weak. His hope makes him believe that something still matters. That belief gives him the courage to face his toughest situations and find solutions.

Also, in the movie, he shares a great message about hope: "Hope is a good thing, maybe the best of things, and no good thing ever dies."

My Mother: A Lesson in Hope

I am very close to my mother. She is a simple homemaker yet the strongest person I know. She finds joy in small kindnesses—distributing food at NGOs, listening without judgment or helping a friend with something.

She was also my father's safe space during vulnerable moments.

Then, five years ago, my world changed.

She was diagnosed with Ataxia, a degenerative disease.

With time, she started needing support to walk. Then, she struggled to even hold her phone and eat on her own. Within a year, she became completely dependent on others.

But she never complained.

She refused to see herself as sick. If someone called her unwell, she'd get angry.

The doctors told us her brain was shrinking every day, yet she had a lot of old memories alive.

She still made a broad smile like a child for the photos.

She still asked for her favourite sweets.

She still wanted her favourite 'Satya Paul' saree, even though she could never wear it.

Was this delusional?

No. The visiting doctor never thought so.

She simply refused to let go of hope.

What Kept Her So Strong?

Then I realised—it wasn't about the body. It was her mindset.

She did not see herself as being less capable.

She kept her hopes alive for the people she loved.

She never talked about pain or past grudges. Rather, she was curious about what was happening around her, the way she always was.

She is probably still hoping that something interesting is there in the coming moments.

Hope Can Feel Like a Gamble

This might sound bizarre but Hope can sometimes feel like a gamble—a leap of faith or moving into the unknown.

When an organisation hires a new employee, or a couple gets married, they do so with hope—believing it is the right decision. Yet, both situations carry the possibility of separation.

But without this hopeful speculation, neither the relationship nor the opportunity would exist in the first place.

Hope when feeling vulnerable leads to courage for being prepared to face all outcomes.

Hope is not an emotion—it is a state of mind

Knowing that it is a state of mind and not an emotion, anyone can inculcate it for life. But how does it make any difference?

If Hope was Just an Emotion, it would be fleeting, like happiness or sadness. Besides, it would be a derivative of external world like good news brings hope and bad news takes it away.

But hope, as a state of mind, becomes our intention. It makes us strong by not getting influenced by the challenges.

Cultivating Hope

Hope is not binary—either 1 or 0. It exists on a spectrum, and we have the power to give it a value and cultivate it ourselves. And there are ways of doing it.

Let me share a scene from the award-winning movie The Pursuit of Happyness. In one scene, the father is playing basketball with his son who dreams of becoming a great player. But the father unknowingly discourages his son by saying that he himself was never good at basketball, so his son may not be either.

But he quickly reframes his message and says that we should never let someone tell us that we can't do something; we have to protect our dreams and should just go for it.

This shift of words made a life-changing difference for his son.

At times, the way we frame our thoughts and words can shape our hopes.

Instead of *saying, "This may not work,"* saying, *"What if it works out?"* can build endless hope.

Even random things can spark hope. A subtle positive thought from a rainbow, sunshine, or even a little bird can build a sense of possibility. Sometimes, it is about just one moment that makes people believe that things would get better.

For me, even resonating music can create hope or, at the very least, add to resilience.

Sometimes, we can borrow hope from an inspirational real-life story, a friend who believes in us, or even the resilience of others around us.

To sum up, we can nurture, redefine, and rediscover hope. It exists in the courage to move forward and our ability to find meaning even in difficult moments. It will always be there as long as we can hold onto even the tiniest spark of hope.

Self Empathy

When was the last time you were genuinely kind to yourself?

It is a simple question, but some people may find it unfair or even uncomfortable to ask or answer.

But the truth is, we are often our own toughest critics. Studies have shown it repeatedly: we have inner dialogues that could be judgemental, and we also keep replaying our mistakes in mind.

And yet, whether we feel vulnerable or not, we all need self-empathy. It is simply about giving ourselves the same patient hearing we offer others.

The Power of Self Empathy

The award-winning movie A Beautiful Mind beautifully shares the power of self-empathy and how it can be life-changing. The actor, a brilliant mathematician is having a mental illness, but he chooses not to be self-judgmental or critical. With self-empathy, he works with his challenges, accepting and understanding them with compassion.

This film is an exceptional watch. It discusses how self-empathy can empower us to accept vulnerabilities with kindness and how it can lead to strength and resilience.

The most powerful emotion

If someone asks you—*what is the most powerful emotion? What would you say?* —I would say **love**. Because love keeps us meaningfully alive, not just in our relationships with others but also within ourselves.

And love cannot exist without empathy.

It is not limited to humans but to everyone around us.

For example, we love having a dog in the family and taking care of it like parents. While dogs can't speak, we look after them with empathy, and in return, we get their unconditional love.

Now, if we show the same empathy with ourselves, we can avoid being harsh with our emotions.

We accept ourselves while we work for bigger things.

Let me tell you a quick story.

I had a frustrating experience with a vendor who was supposed to deliver a Washing machine on a particular day. I followed up multiple times while he showed no urgency or accountability. Rather, he was very casual about it. This led to lot of sufferings as existing machine was not working.

Finally, I just had to have that tough conversation. I was more than firm, maybe even a little blunt. And later? I felt awful thinking I overdid it.

Then, as I reflected, I realised that I had been patient and reacted only after his careless reply and attitude.

This self empathy helped me to be fair to myself and not be harsh.

Self-empathy changes everything.

I have seen leaders with self-empathy say things like, 'I tried my best, but it did not work out. Maybe I need to sit and reflect on everything.' and not, 'I didn't have enough resources and support, which led to where we are.'

They would rather tell themselves when on tough ground, 'I have been through such situations a few times and presently just need to use the same rigour and focus.'

Self-empathy inspires for positive actions, seeking help, or even taking a break.

We might still have questions to ask. Can a Vulnerable Person Have Self-Empathy?

I would say absolutely.

But it comes with effort, attention, and practice, just like an attitude of gratitude or forgiveness.

A vulnerable mind could result from many reasons we have already discussed.

Being mindful of thoughts and emotions and questioning them could help. Just like in the movie A Beautiful Mind.'

Because when we stop fighting ourselves, we finally create the space to grow.

A vulnerable person may initially struggle with self-empathy, but with time, it becomes easier. They no longer see vulnerability as a weakness but a part of their journey. And, while self-empathy helps them deal with challenges, it doesn't mean they have to do it alone—they can always seek support from others.

Trust

In a real sense, trust isn't just about feeling safe.

It is about stepping into the uncertainty, taking a leap of faith, and hoping you will land safely.

But the real question: Can someone who feels vulnerable still find trust in their own self?

I would say—Absolutely.

In fact, vulnerability and trust often go hand in hand.

In difficult and vulnerable situations, we need to take a breath and move forward, trusting ourselves, others, or something greater. It takes courage and self-awareness. We also need to know that anything can happen and trust that we will handle that, too.

So, where does trust start from? With yourself.

Trusting Yourself First

Let's talk about a scene from the powerful movie that excels in sharing this.

The Dark Knight Rises.

In one scene of the movie, the actor is trapped in a deep underground prison. He tries to escape again and again using a safety rope tied around his waist, but he fails every single time and falls back into the prison.

Then, another prisoner gives him a talk – 'You keep using the rope because you're afraid of falling. And that fear is holding you back.

Think about that for a moment. He was failing not because he wasn't strong enough—but because he didn't trust himself.

So, what does he do? He takes a deep breath, removes the rope—the very thing meant to "protect" him—and takes the leap of faith. This time, he makes it.

Why? Because he chose to trust himself more than his fear.

That's the power of self-trust.

The Fastest Way to Trust Yourself

Here's a shortcut—connect with your values.

Think about it: What have you always believed in? Maybe it's honesty, courage, taking risks, or standing up for others.

When in self-doubt, lean into those values. They have always been part of you, why would they fail you now?

But what if no core value comes to mind? That's okay. You can choose one today. Maybe it is resilience, integrity, or even just showing up for yourself. The moment you commit to it, it becomes you guiding values.

And if trusting yourself feels impossible, take a step back. Look at your past. Find proof.

Maybe you don't trust yourself to execute a job now but recall the moments when you did something right, the times when you figured things out, even when you thought you wouldn't.

Finding Trust Through a Larger Purpose

Another way to rebuild trust is to take a moment, maybe close your eyes, take a deep breath, and reconnect with your larger goals. As you open your eyes, the self-doubt may not be there.

Maybe ask yourself: 'What makes this important for me?'

When Nothing Else Works—Trust in Something Bigger

Sometimes, self-trust feels out of reach. We try everything, but the doubts stay with us. The past experiences or the "what-ifs" make it messy.

In those moments, trusting in God—or someone who inspires you—can be the helping hand we need.

Think about the times when you prayed, hoped, or wished for clarity, and somehow—against all odds—things fell into place. Maybe not immediately or in the way you expected, but looking back, you can see how the dots connected.

Faith leads to trust

It reminds us that we're part of something bigger. Our challenges have some meaning, and we are not alone.

Still Struggling? Find out what's Holding You Back.

From Trusting Yourself to Trusting Others

Here's the truth: Once you trust yourself, trusting others becomes easier.

It's about taking a risk—not blindly, but with intention. It's about reminding yourself that people you trust are a better bet than those you don't. And it's about knowing that you are strong enough to handle the outcome no matter what happens.

Because trust isn't about being certain. It's about being brave.

And that? Changes everything.

References

https://pmc.ncbi.nlm.nih.gov/articles/PMC9777048/#:~:text=Conceptually%2C%20psychological%20vulnerability%20(PV),%E2%80%9D%20%5B9%5D%20(p.

https://www.indiatoday.in/education-today/gk-current-affairs/story/battle-of-saragarhi-21-sikhs-stood-against-10000-afghans-2598570-2024-09-12

https://beunlimitable.com/the-science-behind-self-doubt-whats-happening-in-your-brain/?utm_source=chatgpt.com

Credit to the entire team who made such exceptionally great movies

https://www.imdb.com/title/tt1093370/ Jab we met

https://www.imdb.com/title/tt0499375/ Guru

https://www.imdb.com/title/tt0078418/ Trishul

https://www.imdb.com/title/tt0167404/ The sixth sense

https://www.imdb.com/title/tt0072860/ Deewar

https://www.imdb.com/title/tt0250043/ Todasa Roomani Ho jayen

https://www.imdb.com/title/tt2181931/ English Vinglish

https://www.imdb.com/title/tt0073707/ Sholay

https://www.imdb.com/title/tt0903747/ Breaking Bad

https://www.imdb.com/title/tt0454876/ Life of Pi

https://www.imdb.com/title/tt0162222/ Cast away

https://www.imdb.com/title/tt0119217/ Good will Hunting

https://www.imdb.com/title/tt0248126/ Kabhi Khushi Kabhi Gham

https://www.imdb.com/title/tt0112870/ Dilwale Dulhania Le jayenge

https://www.imdb.com/title/tt0111161/ The Shawshank redemption

https://www.imdb.com/title/tt0454921/ The pursuit of happyness.

https://www.imdb.com/title/tt3322420/ Queen

https://www.imdb.com/title/tt0266543/ Finding Nemo

https://www.imdb.com/title/tt0102258/ Lamhe

https://www.imdb.com/title/tt0066070/ Mera naam Joker

https://www.imdb.com/name/nm8113831/ Taare Zameen par

https://www.imdb.com/title/tt0374887/ Munna Bhai MBBS

https://www.imdb.com/title/tt0145487/ Spiderman

https://www.imdb.com/title/tt0169102/ Lagaan

https://www.imdb.com/title/tt1187043/ 3 Idiots

https://www.imdb.com/title/tt0268978/ A beautiful mind

https://www.imdb.com/title/tt1345836/ The dark knight rises

www.ingramcontent.com/pod-product-compliance
Lightning Source LLC
Chambersburg PA
CBHW031134130726
47988CB00006B/2373